D1276164

DISCARDED BY HUNTER LIBRARY WCU

DISCARDED BY HUNTER LIBRARY, WCU

LEONTIEV

nicolas berdyaev

ACADEMIC INTERNATIONAL

LEONTIEV

THE RUSSIAN SERIES Volume 15

LEONTIEV

nicolas berdyaev

ACADEMIC INTERNATIONAL/orbis academicus
ORONO ● MAINE ● 04473   1968

RUSSIAN SERIES / VOLUME 15

Nicolas Berdyaev, LEONTIEV

Original Title: KONSTANTIN LEONT'EV. OCHERK IZ
ISTORII RUSSKOI RELIGIOZNOI MYSLI. Paris, 1926

Reprinted from the first English language edition, London, 1940

Translated from the Russian by George Reavy

Printed in the United States of America

Library of Congress Catalog Number: 68-56360

Orders should be addressed directly to

ACADEMIC INTERNATIONAL

ORONO • MAINE • 04473

HUNTER LIBRARY
WESTERN CAROLINA UNIVERSITY

B
4249
.L44
B42
1968

PREFACE TO THE ENGLISH EDITION

In the Preface to the French edition of this book, I have clearly explained my attitude to Constantine Leontiev; but I should like to emphasize once again that I am personally more than ever in disagreement with those who base their appreciation of values not on the human personality, but on ideas that coerce and transform human personality into a means to an end. That was the substance and value of Leontiev's religious and social philosophy.

NICOLAS BERDYAEV

PREFACE

It is some eighteen years since I wrote this book. I had long been fascinated by the extraordinary personality and tragic destiny of this thinker. As it happens, I did devote an article to him in 1905—one of the first, I think, to give a general survey of his character and work.

I cannot claim to have written an 'objective' study, for that term is meaningless as far as I am concerned; but I have written in a spirit of great sympathy for Leontiev. This sympathy may appear strange, for I by no means share Leontiev's ideas; and my social and religious philosophy is not only very different from, but is also opposed to, his. But in my eyes, Leontiev's destiny is profoundly moving; and he is one of the great nineteenth-century Russians, one of the representative figures in the history of the Russian spirit.

As a sociologist and an historical philosopher, Leontiev predicted many events with a startling perspicacity. His ideology belongs no doubt to the past, but he forecast the character of our age so precisely and so comprehensively, that he can claim some affinity with our times.

Constantine Leontiev is the Russian precursor of Nietzsche, and he ended his days in a monastery. Actually he ignored the existence of Nietzsche, but he had many things in common with him: his aesthetic passion for destiny, his cult of force and aspiration for power, his aristocratism and vital tension—his way of basing the hierarchy of values on violence. He is also Nietzschean in his would-be amoralism, in his love for a flourishing culture, in his fear of cultural decadence, in his taste for cruelty placed at the service of the highest values, in his Renaissance attitude.

Leontiev clearly perceived that human societies would not be able to survive on the basis of the humanitarian principle, that they must relapse into a state of bloody dictatorship. He foresaw both Communism and Fascism. His presentiment did not betray him, when he denounced the 'process of simplifying confusion', which was undermining the social structure and helping to lower cultural values. He was also the precursor of Spengler, in so far as the latter posed the problem of 'the decline of nations' and established a distinction between culture and civilization.

Leontiev was horrified to see that culture was being transformed into a uniform mechanical civilization. His suggested method of counteracting this fatal process was no doubt erroneous, because purely reactionary, and he himself admitted the sterility of his method.

He believed neither in the freedom of the spirit nor in the value and dignity of the human personality. He could not accept with equanimity the inroads of Democracy, which held no truth for him. He looked upon the struggle to preserve cultural values without any great hope, at least, as long as the democratic process was rampant.

He predicted the end of the world. But actually he meant the end of an historic epoch, the end of the Russian Empire. His view of the relations between Christianity and the world was an extremely dualistic one. For although he believed in the mission of Christianity and in the salvation it brought to the individual soul, he never attempted to defend it from the social and historical standpoint.

Frenchmen will no doubt discover certain affinities between Leontiev and Joseph de Maistre, Gobineau and, in our day, Charles Maurras, although it is improbable that Maurras would ever enter a monastery, as Leontiev did towards the end of his life. He also differs from Maurras in his bitter criticism of nationalism.

There are, indeed, to be found in Leontiev decisive arguments against nationalism and racialism, and he is certainly not half-hearted in his denunciation of these principles. But the most remarkable facts about him are his personality and destiny.

His failure lies in his refusal to understand the dignity of every human personality as an image and likeness of God, despite the fact that he was dominated by the religious sentiment of sin (a feeling which sometimes inspired terror) and by the aesthetic feeling of beauty. He had no conception of the dignity and freedom of the spirit, or of the historic sins of the Church on the social plane. Leontiev's ideas would prove harmful in our day, but his life and history are highly instructive.

NICOLAS BERDYAEV

CONTENTS

[xi]

CHAPTER I

LEONTIEV'S ORIGINS AND YOUTH IN MOSCOW. HIS NATURALISM AND AESTHETICISM. LOVE. HIS LITERARY DÉBUT. SERVICE IN THE CRIMEA. THE QUEST OF HAPPINESS THROUGH BEAUTY

I

Constantine Leontiev was an exceptional and unique person, and to love and appreciate him would require a special predilection. As Rozanov has said so well of him, 'Just as he had no precursors—*all* Slavophils were not his precursors—so he founded no school. I know that at the present time he has no more than two or three faithful disciples—twenty or thirty would be too many—either in this country or in all cultured lands; and it is very likely he will never have any more. I mean, of course, devoted admirers of his cult and work, those who prefer his *literary type* to all others, Russian or foreign.' It is difficult to place Leontiev; he does not fit into the main current of Russian social thought. He was not allied to any particular school, he founded none himself; he was not typical of any one age or tendency. He had neither precursors nor disciples. He took part in the political controversies of his time, and wrote a great deal on topical themes; but, although his exceptional talent was generally admitted, he exercised very little influence in his day. He remained misunderstood and unpopular, a solitary thinker and recluse.

In his almost vituperative articles on current political questions he stated his most personal thoughts, forebodings and visions. His manner of treating eternal problems in terms of contemporary life was highly disconcerting and incomprehensible to the conservative camp to which he was officially and formally most nearly affiliated, while at the same time it was unpalatable to the liberal parties. Rozanov again has admirably summed up this position: 'The Westerners abhor him, while the Slavophils are afraid of welcoming him into their midst. This singular position is in itself an indication that we have to do with an original, powerful and great intelligence, one that has not as yet been properly assessed in the history of Russian literature. . . .'

The will to power, the cult of power, were the essential inspiration of Leontiev's work. But, like Nietzsche, he was in private life the most powerless of men, enjoying the aesthetic delights of power but not actual power itself. He was an aesthete, the first Russian aesthete, in an age when Russian thought was essentially social; and for that reason he found himself isolated, misunderstood and ignored. A close examination of Leontiev's character and destiny would suggest as the reason for his ostracism the fact that he had many traits which ran counter to Russian sentiment, character and outlook on life. In one of his letters he stated that *he was concerned less with suffering humanity than with poetic humanity*. This indifference to 'suffering humanity', this exaltation of 'poetic humanity' at its expense, must have appeared strange, and even repugnant, to the majority of the Russia intelligentsia. Leontiev was not a humanist, or if he was, he was certainly more spiritually akin to the sixteenth-century Italian type. His pronounced and militant aestheticism gave him the air of being a foreigner in Russian society. There was no purely aesthetic movement in Russian thought until the beginning of the twentieth century, and even then the aesthetic attitude was imitative rather than spontaneous, an expression of intellectualism rather than of deep-rooted necessity.

Leontiev was also a romantic. But Romanticism was an entirely Western phenomenon, of Catholic and Protestant origin, completely alien to the Orthodox East. Similarly, Russians were almost strangers to the cult of love which Leontiev had revived. His thought, too, was latin in its precision and clarity; there was nothing vague or vapid in his writing. His mind worked like that of a psychologist or a physiologist, and this again alienated him from his Russian readers. Moreover, Leontiev was an aristocrat by nature: his character, his feeling for life, his convictions were all aristocratic. That was another non-Russian trait in him, for Russians are at bottom democrats, and resent the claims of aristocracy. The Slavophils were typical Russian gentry and landowners, but there was nothing aristocratic about them. In fact, aristocratism is a Western phenomenon. Almost all Russian writers and thinkers became engrossed in popular and democratic ideas, and these ideas were almost as common among right wing writers as among left wing ones. Leontiev was quite impervious to these enthusiasms; his soul was never captivated by the love of the people or by democratic ideas. In this respect he can only be compared with Tchaadayev, who also found himself isolated and ignored.

But the paradox of Leontiev's peculiar position was that he nevertheless endeavoured to interpret the Russian spirit. Hence he was often regarded, though erroneously, as an ad-

[3]

herent of the Slavophil cause. But he was not a Slavophil: he was, indeed, in many ways totally opposed to that creed. Neither was he a Westerner like Tchaadayev. As we have already indicated, he belonged to no movement and professed no accepted doctrine. He had none of the characteristic traits of a Slavophil or a Westerner. He was a solitary spirit, a man of absolutely unique destiny. He was one of those remarkable beings who are concerned exclusively with the problem of their personal destiny, and experience no necessity to act, to serve their fellow-beings or to pursue any definite objective. Leontiev was preoccupied solely with himself in relation to eternity. That accounts for his restlessness, his constant change of profession, his inability to find any peace. That explains, too, why he was in turn doctor, consul, man of letters, censorship official and, lastly, monk. He treated external problems as if they were part of his private destiny. The style of his life, of his writings, was wholly objective. In fact, the objective and the subjective aspects of life were for him synonymous. For that reason, he was a particularly interesting type of man. Here is a passage in which he describes his youthful aspirations: 'I was twenty-three; my imagination and my heart were the rulers of my life. I searched for poetry everywhere; but I not only searched for it, I also *succeeded in finding it*. I longed for all sorts of adventures, work, pleasures, dangers, a life of intrepid battles and poetic leisure.'

Leontiev's life falls into two periods : that preceding his religious crisis of 1871, and that following it. In both these periods the problem of his personal destiny was his chief concern. In the first period, he attempted to find happiness in Beauty, in the *ultrabiological* sphere, in *vital tension*. In the second period, he confined himself to the quest of personal salvation. *First aesthetic ecstasy, then religious terror in face of damnation*: these were the ruling impulses of Leontiev's life. The instinct of *struggling with death* and that of *immortal beauty* were equally active throughout these periods of his life.

II

National, social, and family traditions and instincts all help to determine man's unique and inimitable individuality, and to form him. A man's hereditary traits, his origins, his childhood myths and environment are not accidental acquisitions from which he should or can hope to free himself entirely; they are profound ties shaping his destiny. It was not by chance that Leontiev was born a Russian of gentle blood. Far from being an accident, his ancestry was the very kernal of his life. It would be difficult to imagine him as anything but a *barin* or gentleman. In his outward appearance, as well as in his spiritual essence, Leontiev was unmistakably a scion of the gentry. If we were to ignore his aristocratic origins, we should fail to understand his destiny or to grasp his outlook on the world. Spiritually he was representative of his country and his race. Men of great creative powers transcend their race and environment, but these latter are the soil which has helped to nourish and educate them. It is hard to form an idea of Leon Tolstoy without taking into account his background, that of the landed gentry, against which he reacted violently. A noble may rebel against his aristocratic environment, a *barin* may criticize and attack his fellow-*barins*, but he will do so in the manner of a noble or *barin*. Thus, to his dying day, Tolstoy remained a *barin* in his negation, just as Leontiev remained one in his affirmation.

Constantine Leontiev was born on the 13th of January, 1831, on the Kudinovo estate, in the Mestchov district of the government of Kaluga. He used to say that, like Vladimir Solovyev, he was born a seven months' child. His father had no outstanding gifts and had very little influence on his son. Like many of the gentry he had served as an officer in a guards regiment. It would appear that he had been cashiered from his regiment for a breach of discipline. Thereafter he had settled down to live on his estate. In his *Memoirs*, Leontiev spoke of his father with scant respect: 'My father was one of those old-fashioned Russian nobles who were unable to concentrate their attention on anything, and who had no sense of discipline. On the whole, my father was neither intelligent nor serious.' Leontiev received the news of his father's death with complete indifference. There are certain grounds for believing that he was a natural son. His mother would seem to have been the focus of all Leontiev's childhood impressions and feelings. She appears to have been superior to her husband in every respect, and it is even hard to understand why she should have married a man whose gifts were so inferior to hers. His mother came of a family of gentry, the Karabanovs. Writing about his maternal grandfather, Leontiev said: 'He was, perhaps, one of the most typical representatives of that old Russian nobility which was sometimes an attractive and, at other times, a revolting blend of French refinement and Asiatic cruelty and savagery. He carried himself like a *grand seigneur*; he was handsome and excessively aloof; capable of chivalrous and lofty impulses; he detested falsehood, prevarication and equivocation. There was no doubt about his courage: he once attacked the provincial governor sword in hand because the latter had dared

[6]

to disbelieve him. A faithful servant of the Tsar, a patriot, loyal and energetic, a lover of poetry and beauty, he was at the same time despotic to the point of madness, depraved to the point of crime, suspicious to the point of absurdity, and cruel to the point of bestiality.' A grandfather such as this must have made a strong impression on Leontiev, and some of his characteristics were transmitted to his grandson. He, too, was a blend of refinement and ferocity, but in a much milder degree.

As we have already noted, his mother's image played a preponderant part in his childhood impressions and memories. His first aesthetic and religious impulses were associated with her; for the awakening of his religious feelings went hand in hand with that of his aesthetic sensibility, which his elegant and pretty mother had done much to stimulate. As he said himself, 'When I remember those days, I recapture the feelings I then experienced. I can see the room in which my mother worked, the striped tricoloured divan on which, on awakening, I used to recline lazily. A winter morning; through the window I could see our garden all covered with snow. In a corner of the room, I can remember my sister reading a psalm aloud: "Have mercy upon me, O God!" "Purge me with hyssop, and I shall be clean: wash me, and I shall be whiter than snow." "The sacrifices of God *are* a broken spirit: a broken and contrite heart, O God, Thou wilt not despise." I have remembered these words ever since, and they gave me great pleasure. For some reason they moved me deeply. . . . At the age of forty, when my mother was no longer among the living, when after a succession of spiritual crises I wished once more to learn to believe, and visited the Russian monks in Mount Athos, the memory of those

[7]

morning prayers at home, in the mahogany study with its window looking out on the snow-covered garden, the memory of the words of that psalm still filled me with a remote but familiar, loving and warm glow. The poetry of religious impressions helps me to nourish the love of religion. And love can kindle again the heart of a dying faith. "The sacrifices of God are a broken spirit: a broken and a contrite heart, O God, Thou wilt not despise." '

'Since then I have never been able to think of my mother or of my country without remembering that passage from the psalm; nor can I listen to it without remembering my mother, my young sister, our dear Kudinovo, the beautiful and spacious garden and the view from the window of that room. In winter as well as in summer, when the flower-beds were full of blooming roses, that view filled my heart with an ineffable poetry which strangers would hardly understand.' From his childhood days, too, Leontiev had an aesthetic love for the Orthodox liturgy, and that love was destined one day to play an important *rôle* in his religious conversion.

Leontiev's first definite aesthetic impressions are bound up with his recollection of his mother and of his native Kudinovo estate; they were the source of his early conception of beauty. 'In our dear Kudinovo, in our spacious and joyous home, of which no trace survives to-day, there was a room with windows facing to the West, overlooking a tranquil, leafy and spacious garden. Our house was smart and tidy, but that room appealed to me most of all; for me there was an air of mystery about it which was hardly noticed by the servants, visitors or even the family. It was my mother's study. . . . My mother loved solitude, silence and reading;

she was very meticulous, and kept to a strict time-table in her work. When I was still a child, and "all the impressions of life were still new to me", I was enchanted by that room. . . . My mother was very imaginative, she had great taste.'

'In the summer there was a profusion of flowers every-where, vases of lilac, roses, lily of the valley, wild jasmin; in the winter there was a scent of fine perfume. I remember a handsome cut-glass flagon filled with perfume; it had a sort of gadget attached to it, I did not know what for; nor can I now say what it was for. . . . There was also a twisted wire, and a wick, and somehow it all lit up; the wire became red hot and the room was gradually filled with a persistent, delicate and subtle fragrance. . . . The recollection of my mother's charming "Hermitage" is inextricably bound up in my heart with my very first childhood religious impres-sions, with my early awakening to the beauty of nature, and with the most precious image of my beautiful, elegant and noble mother herself, to whom I owed so much,—my feel-ing of patriotism and monarchy, my love of strict order and unremitting labour, and my refined taste.' According to Leontiev himself, his mother had an austere and irascible character rather than a kindly and tender one. But that did not prevent him from feeling an enduring love towards her, all through his life he never did anything that might offend the sentiments and the ideals in which his mother believed to her dying day. She was a conservative and a monarchist, and her ideals became associated in Leontiev's mind with the image of Beauty. His native Kudinovo, which towards the end of his life he was obliged to sell to the peasants, was also a part of his conception of Beauty. His whole life through he was haunted by the poetic charm and beauty of Russian

[9]

country estates, and he hated anything that might destroy this poetry and beauty. The liberal, equalitarian, and progressive ideas tended, of course, to do away with all those beautiful things which were associated in his mind with the memory of his mother and his home. He always remembered his sister's birthday, and his delight in the wonderful Kudinovo flowers. 'From that moment I had a clear, conscious and lasting perception of the beauties of early spring and summer, a feeling that the flowers in the vase upon the table represented something joyous, young and noble, something exalted. . . . On that morning of the eighteenth of May I experienced all that men have ever thought about flowers. . . . And ever since then I cannot see irises, lilac or narcissus even in a picture, without remembering that morning, that bouquet of flowers, my sister's birthday.' Thus his aestheticism was an early growth, and it became the ruling passion of his life. He was to elaborate a system of aesthetic criteria which he applied to all the phenomena of life. Mount Athos, the Optina monastery, monastic life itself, were all equally powerless to shake the foundations of an aestheticism which was so deep-rooted in his intelligible being.

In his largely autobiographical novel, *Podlypki*, Leontiev evoked the poetry of the nobleman's estate, and attributed to his hero, Ladnev, his own subtle aesthetic experiences. Like Leontiev, Ladnev loved *refinement of feeling*, and was not tempted by anything common and vulgar. But an aesthetic ecstasy and appreciation of life have their reverse side in disillusionment, melancholy and pessimism, in the sense that beauty is thwarted at every step by the ugliness and deformity of life. From his earliest years Leontiev was a prey to these fits of disillusionment, melancholy and pessimism. He did not delude himself with the belief that beauty could ever triumph in the earthly life. Moreover, he had become convinced that, in a general sense, beauty was on the decline, that *so-called progress spelled the death of beauty*. He not only perceived this fact before the French *fin de siècle* 'decadents', symbolists and Catholics, but he also lived this experience in a more tragic way, for he sought after an *aestheticism of life* and could not console himself with an artistic aestheticism, as did Huysmans and others at the time. Thus Ladnev, the hero of his *Podlypki*, who thirsted for love, voluptuousness and ecstasy, was made to exclaim: 'O my God! Is it not better to become an anchoret or a monk,—a resolute and illumined monk who knows his soul's desire, a spirit free and lucid as a fresh autumn day? . . . Is not this bright solitary life better than a stifling marriage, tragically compounded of pity, boredom, the rare flashes of a last evanescing love, children and monotony?' Leontiev seems to have entertained thoughts like these very early on, when he was still a young man. He felt that there was an unbridgeable gulf between romantic love and conjugal or family life. He often returned to the subject; *Podlypki* ends on this note: 'How stuffy everything is! What is the end of even great men? Death. What has life given them? I can see vividly Napoleon, dressed in a frock-coat and with a broad-brimmed hat upon his head, standing with his hands behind his back. . . . In front of him are a lady and a negro staggering under his load. . . . How bored he is! Here is another picture: Madame Bertrand with her high comb, eaten with cancer, her mouth open, and death. I also see Goethe in an old-fashioned coat, married to a cook . . . how stuffy is his room! Schiller is exhausted by nightly labours and dies young; Rousseau is married to Thérèse, who has no idea who her husband is. . . . And these were all great men! Is this not atrocious and horrible in every respect?'

Leontiev began his life as a romantic, but his romanticism was of an austere and ruthless kind, stripped of any 'rosy perspectives'. He was a precursor of the neo-Romantic movement of the end of the nineteenth and beginning of the twentieth century, the first martyr of that spiritual revival, its most serious representative, who did not stop half-way and who pursued his experience to the bitter end. His début in life is excellently described in the words of the hero of his *The Egyptian Dove*: 'After some early successes compatible with my ideals, I fell in love with life and all its irreconcilable contradictions; I came to regard my passionate participation in this variegated drama of earthly existence as an almost sacred mission, and its profound meaning appeared to me to be inexpressibly mysterious and mystically insoluble. Disciplining myself in this struggle, I learned at the same time to enjoy as strongly and as consciously as possible all that destiny brought me. There were few who could extract as much pleasure as I did from roses, while not forgetting for a single instant the pain caused me by the slightest thorn!' This passionate participation in the variegated drama of earthly existence, his attempts to solve its profound and mysterious meaning while plunging ever deeper into its abyss, brought him great disillusionment and suffering. In fact, they awoke in him the terror of damnation and confronted him with the insoluble enigma of being.

III

On finishing school in 1849, Leontiev proceeded to the Iaroslav college; but in the course of the same year he joined the medical faculty of the Moscow University. He did not take up the medical career of his own volition, but rather under the pressure of circumstances, and at his mother's wish. Nor was he destined to practise as a doctor for long; medicine played a very small part in his life as a whole. As a matter of fact, he was not very suited to that profession, but his medical studies left their mark upon him. His training in biology helped to form his mode of thought, so that ever after he had a naturalistic bias. In fact, Leontiev's naturalism was one of the determining elements in his spiritual life, first of all associated with his aestheticism, and later with his religiosity. He remained an anatomist, physiologist and pathologist of human society, employing the analogical method and comparing the process of 'secondary simplification' in human society with pathological processes, such as pneumonia. With this went a Gallic precision and clarity of mind, which rebelled against the more nebulous flights of metaphysics. He felt ill at ease when confronted with German philosophy. Thus, although Leontiev was a remarkable, penetrating and daring thinker, he was not a philosopher either in his training, type of mind, or culture. He had to confess his impotence when faced with the more abstract philosophical problems. He was unable to think in abstract terms; his own expression was clear and concrete, and his thought betrayed his naturalistic and artistic bias. There was something latin in his intellectual type. And it may have been no accident that he embarked upon his early medical studies which were so different from his real vocation. It is clear from Leontiev's work that his training had not been a 'classical' one. And although he mastered his passion for the natural sciences, he remained essentially a realist in all his

[13]

enterprises,—in his social philosophy, in his literary work, in his journalism, and even in his outlook on religious problems. His realism was tempered by a certain romanticism of feeling, but that did not make him an idealist. In fact, his intellectual temperament was the very opposite of Vladimir Solovyev's.

Leontiev's life as a student in Moscow was by no means a gay and happy one. He was often ill and in pecuniary straits; he held himself aloof from his fellow-students and had qualms about the studies he was pursuing. He demanded a great deal from life. He did not set out to probe the meaning of life, but rather to live a full and exalted life—a life full of colour and incident. At the time he had no belief of any kind; and he experienced a period of acute melancholy, so characteristic of young men of talent who find no outlet for their inner turbulence. He has an excellent description of his then state of mind: 'At that time I found life very hard. Everything conspired to make me suffer: want and social vanity, family life, my work in the anatomical theatre on the decomposing bodies of unfortunate and forsaken people, physical ills, my unbelief, the fear that I might go to seed before I had flowered properly, the fear of dying before my time, "*sans avoir connu la passion, sans avoir été aimé*!"' This passage is especially interesting for its revelation of Leontiev's romantic thirst for love, his anticipation of its ecstasies, and his fear of dying before he had lived through this supreme experience. In another passage he confessed that his mother had brought him up somewhat effeminately; and it is true, that there were certain feminine traits in his character. This may appear surprising to those who know Leontiev as a writer of fierce and ruthless invective, but the fact cannot be denied when we penetrate deeper into his personal des-

[14]

tiny. His complex character, the romantic nature of his sentimental life, his militant aestheticism, his inability to settle down in life, his tumultuous aspirations and eternal dissatisfaction, all these characteristics presuppose a feminine side to his nature, the bisexual structure of his soul. The thirst for love, the eternal quest of amorous ecstasy, the inability to find a single, satisfying, truly connubial love, are usually the sign of a complex blend of masculine and feminine principles in a man's nature. They were all true of Leontiev. He attached tremendous importance to beautiful appearance, elegance and physical strength—an indication this of an erotic nature. He was rude in his intercourse with Botkin because the latter's outward appearance displeased him. Like many of the romantic and idealist young men of his day, he was an enthusiastic admirer of George Sand, and she exercised a considerable influence on the development not so much of his thought as of his feelings. Leontiev has said that he was both a romantic and a nihilist in his youth. He has described his youth as a period of 'dreams, ambitions and unbearable torments'. At that time a desperate struggle was being waged within him between his poetic and moral natures. He did not appear to be interested in politics: 'In those years I gave no thought to political questions; I neither understood nor wished to understand them, being preoccupied exclusively with the problems of personal happiness, dignity or poetic encounters, struggle, and adventure.' He was interested in the dramatic and poetic aspects of Revolutions rather than in their attempts to reconstruct society. In short, he was one of those men 'who thought more about the development of their own personality than about assisting their fellow-men'. In this respect he was like Goethe.

[15]

During his stay in Moscow, Leontiev fell in love with a young girl, Zinaida Konova, who reciprocated his affection. Their relationship lasted some five years, and 'went through the most varied phases, from simple friendship to the most ardent passion'. But the relationship was ill-defined and never gave complete satisfaction. This is Leontiev's first love affair about which we have any knowledge; it came to an end on his own initiative, and Zinaida made a marriage of convenience. All his life through Leontiev had great success with women. He was a handsome man. Turgeniev said of him that he was 'an extremely *joli garçon*'; and once told him to his face that, 'with your appearance and gifts, you might drive a lot of women mad if you wished.' Leontiev himself confessed that he was more flattered by his success with women than by any recognition of his talent. Characteristic of this phase of Leontiev's life is the passage in his *Memoirs* in which he draws a comparison between his life and that of Katkov, whose wife was 'a thin woman, with high-set shoulders and a large nose', whose apartment was that of 'a hard-working man', and whose dressing-gown was just 'ordinary'. Leontiev goes on to say: 'After visiting him, I returned to my three spacious and decent rooms, and looking into the mirror I saw there—in the mirror and in everything else—many, very many hopes. . . . The family were no longer with me, thank God! Z. was waiting for me upstairs, in that fine apartment, sitting upon silks, and herself dressed in silk. She was perfumed, clever, affectionate, passionate, self-loving. . . . *Tu demandes, si je t'aime*, she would say. *Ah! je t'adore. . . . Mais non! J'aurais voulu inventer un autre mot. . . .* That's not the same thing as Madame Katkov. . . . Poor Katkov! A respectable man, but so poor. Turgeniev, at least, is a bachelor, a very handsome man, a *bel homme*, a *barin* with two thousand serfs. . . . That's another matter.' Leontiev himself advised Zinaida to get married. He 'sacrificed his love for the sake of freedom and art'. 'He sacrificed both youthful passion and his hopes of tranquil domestic happiness with such a clever and affectionate woman for the sake of the unknown future of poetry, adventure and fame!' As a matter of fact, Leontiev was afraid of marriage and married life. He wished to retain his freedom, his poetry, which were threatened by domestic happiness, children, and so on. He was prepared to sacrifice his happiness and personal love for the sake of the creative life. The romantic side of his nature stopped short of realizing his dream. He broke off relations not only with the woman he loved, but also with a great friend of his, a certain Georgievsky whom he described as one of the ablest of men, a genius almost. He did so as soon as he felt that his freedom was endangered, that he was becoming too dependent on him, that he was embarrassed by his trying criticisms. He wished to be absolutely free and alone to pursue a violent, varied and beautiful life. Like most romantics, he believed that the future held for him some great, unique and beautiful experience; and that he must remove all obstacles in its way.

IV

Leontiev's nature and gifts were essentially those of an artist. His thwarted creative aspirations, his languor and melancholy, were all to find an expression in art. As in the case of many creative thinkers, his aspirations failed to realize themselves in life but found expression in literature. It was under the pressure of life's cruel sufferings that Leon-

[17]

tiev finally became conscious of his artistic vocation. His first literary work was a comedy entitled *The Love Marriage*, written in 1851. He was twenty-one at the time. As he himself has said, that work was founded upon a penetrating analysis of morbid sentiments. Leontiev decided to show his first literary efforts to Turgeniev. He had already had the opportunity of meeting Khomyakov and Pogodin, but he had little love for these writers. But he did appreciate Turgeniev's talent and was, indeed, influenced by him. In his memoirs entitled, *My Literary Relations with Turgeniev*, Leontiev has left us a very interesting analysis of the feelings animating him when he paid a visit to the author of *A Nest of Gentlefolk*. The aesthetic and aristocratic mannerism of the literary *debutant* are here much in evidence: 'I knew nothing of Turgeniev's outward appearance and worldly position, and I was afraid of meeting a man who might be *incapable of being a hero*. I was afraid of being ushered into the presence of an ugly, modest and poor man, in a word, of a wretched hack whose very aspect would be enough to poison my inner sores. From my childhood I hated mediocrity, boredom, everything *petit bourgeois* and plebeian.' Leontiev goes on to tell of his visit to Turgeniev and of his first impressions. His aesthetic apprehensions were dissipated: 'He had beautiful hands, *des mains soignées*, large manly hands. . . .' 'He was a true *barin*!' Turgeniev impressed the young man as being 'much more *heroic* than his heroes'.

Turgeniev was the first to appreciate Leontiev's literary gifts. He took the young man under his wing and did a great deal to help him. 'Your work is essentially morbid but nevertheless excellent,' such was Turgeniev's reaction to *The Love Marriage*. He played an important part in Leontiev's

[18]

melancholy and painful youth, and helped to illumine the young man's life. 'Turgeniev had a lot to do with my enlightenment,' wrote Leontiev. 'He placed his knowledge at my disposal, and raised me above myself; yes, that is the right word, he *raised me up*. It was very necessary at the time, if only to put me properly on my feet. My two previous years of study had been very trying. I was perplexed by the lack of understanding on the part of my fellow-beings, by the material conditions of my life, by the first symptoms of carnal desire suddenly afflicting me, and by the whirlpool of *my mind which was undergoing its first profound metamorphosis*.'

Turgeniev attempted to get Leontiev's work accepted in reviews. But the censorship forbade its publication—a measure of which Leontiev was himself to approve later. Nevertheless the young man's first attempts had some success. Krayevsky advised him to write as much as possible, while Katkov showed every good-will. How different was this happy literary *début* from the contempt and lack of comprehension which greeted him in his maturity, when he wrote his best pages! It was with warm gratitude that he recalled later the memory of Turgeniev. It was largely owing to the latter that he broke off relations with his best friend, Georgyievsky, whose acid criticisms tried his patience too much.

After *The Love Marriage*, Leontiev wrote an unfinished novel, *The Boulavin Mill*. The censorship put difficulties in the way of its publication. Discussing the project of this novel in his *Memoirs*, he wrote: 'The Censor was right to prevent the publication of *The Boulavin Mill* as I had originally planned it in my leisure years.' The subject was in the highest degree immoral, above all in its erotic aspect. . . . At that time he was already beginning to be conscious of the idea 'that there is nothing absolutely immoral, and that everything is moral or immoral only *aesthetically*'. . . . 'This idea that the criterion of *everything* should not be moral but aesthetic, and that Nero himself is more kin to me, more precious, than any mediocre, simple and good person,—this idea, I say, which was the foundation of my outlook on the world from the age of twenty-five to that of forty,—had from that moment begun to penetrate my work. . . .' Leontiev became definitively aware of his vocation as a writer, and this awareness tempered his melancholy. But he remained dissatisfied with his manner of writing; he felt that he was not bold enough, that he dared not be entirely himself, that he suffered from a false sense of shame. He aspired 'to write a work of genius; a work that would be sincere to the point of shamelessness, but perfect. You will die, but your work will persist.' He was conscious of the contradictions between science and art. His University studies were drawing to an end, a crisis was in the offing, and that crisis was to find a solution in a sudden change affecting his outward life—a change which he gladly welcomed.

V

The Crimean War led to a general mobilization of doctors. This enabled Leontiev to take his medical degree before he had quite completed his studies; and at his own request he was drafted into the army as a military surgeon. In August, 1854, he went to Kerstch where he was attached to a hospital. Later on he was transferred to Yenikale. His whole life was transformed: he suddenly found himself leading a very different and more natural life. He moved about among primitive uneducated men and perhaps for the first time he learned to enjoy life. In the Crimea he threw off his melancholy and sense of impotence; he developed in many ways and became more virile. 'When I recalled my student years, my former misanthropy, I no longer recognized myself. I had become healthy, energetic, alert; I was more cheerful, calmer, firmer, and more daring; even my literary setbacks failed to disturb my equilibrium, my almost mystical faith in my stars.' He looked upon his life at Kerstch as a sort of tonic. Leontiev—the poet, thinker, artist—was quite content to call himself simply a 'hospital warden'. The fact that he was unknown, that his *amour propre* was not involved, helped to put him at his ease. For the first time he was able to enjoy an exotic life quite different from that of Moscow and Kaluga. 'A sweet joy filled my soul. . . . The country was quite new to me, it was wild and picturesque; the hills alternatively green and arid hemmed in a large strait; and the girls, Greek or Armenian, were beautiful. Fresh acquaintanceships. Solitary walks along the rocks, over the mournful steppe, along the quays lit by a full winter moon. The wretched Tartar hovels. . . . The remembrance of a passion that had not yet died, of my mother now so far away, of my native Russia.' He was horrified and ashamed to recall that, in Moscow, 'he was sick with love and thinking, that he was in the throes of lofty and refined sufferings.' 'On seeing myself in a mirror, I realized how much the rude and active life I was leading had changed me physically: I looked fresh, pink and young enough to be twenty. . . . I was highly delighted and almost in love with my venal colleagues who did not give a damn for anything "refined" or "lofty"!'

Leontiev had many love affairs in the Crimea. But one of these, to all appearance as superficial as the others, was to have fatal consequences upon his life, for it led to his marrying a woman with whom he had nothing in common. Leontiev's whole life was full of a variety of romances which did not affect him deeply or leave any imprint upon his spiritual life. He never met his ideal companion, the woman of his dreams. He was passionate, but his eroticism was not of the delicate kind. He knew the vulgar Aphrodite too well, and the heavenly Aphrodite too little. This fact had a determining influence upon his spiritual life, and it partly explained his strictly monastic, ascetic, austere and joyless type of religiosity. Thus, unlike Vladimir Solovyev who aspired to find a Heavenly Companion, Leontiev was not a deep-rooted romantic in the domain of love. His eroticism was exclusively earthly and pagan; and he was the first to oppose it to his Christianity. Whereas Solovyev fused his eroticism with his Christianity, there is no trace of the cult of the eternal feminine in Leontiev, no trace of the 'Sophia' who had become a symbol for a whole generation of writers. Leontiev's attitude had been clear from the beginning; he did not change it even when he became a monk. It was characteristic of Leontiev's whole life, that he was never able to concentrate on a single object of love, a single calling, a single place of residence, or a single friend or circle of friends. He was a wanderer in this world, and he found no haven of rest until he had settled down in the Optina monastery.

In the lyrical and tender letters he wrote to his mother from the Crimea, Leontiev complained of his lack of material means. This want of money was to dog him for the rest of his life. It was a great trial for a man of his aristocratic instincts, of his aesthetic outlook with its insistence upon the plastic beauty of the environment, of his unsuitability for any kind of salaried profession. His aestheticism was above all of the pictorial and plastic type. Incarnated beauty and splendour were essential to him; their lack, ugly or tasteless surroundings, were a torture to him. Thus, in writing to his mother, he said: 'When I remember that I shall soon be twenty-five, and that I am still living in want and unable to dress decently, then I cannot help feeling a little sad; when I remember all the setbacks I have experienced in my literary work, and borne with equanimity, all the quarrels and un-pleasantnesses in the past, then I want to work so as to get at least a thousand roubles a year as soon as possible.' But the letters Leontiev wrote as an old man towards the end of his life echo the same complaints. He shared the difficulties of his material position with many eminent men. He loved the pomp and glitter of wealth, but in the pursuit of some higher end Providence condemned him to comparative poverty. He was obliged to earn his living although he had nothing but contempt for the working type of man, the symbol to him of the bourgeois life. He loved the outward luxuries of life, but was too disinterested to profit by life's opportunities; and like many exceptional men he was destined to live a solitary and misunderstood life. In this we may detect the working of a mysterious higher principle.

Leontiev's uneventful stay in Yenikale began to bore him. The peaceful occupation of a military surgeon behind the front did not appeal to him. He was anxious to play a more active part in the war itself. He was eager for adventure and violent impressions. In this he resembled those young Russions of the 1820's who flocked to the Caucasus in the hope that the Caucasian wars might satisfy their thirst for action and picturesque life, and palliate their boredom with a quiet and uniform civilized life. That was, of course, a romantic trait. Leontiev never got over his love and idealization of war, in which he saw an antidote to modern bourgeois civilization. For the same reason he admired Oriental bandits. He had no liking for literary groups and kept aloof from them. 'My own kind and the people, *les deux extrèmes*, have always appealed to me more than the middle, professorial, and literary circle of society which I was obliged to frequent in Moscow. I should have preferred to be on horseback. . . . But where is there a horse in Moscow? I wanted the forest, in winter even. But where is it? None of the *literati* or *savants* pleased me *personally* from the point of view of company or of life. I looked upon them all as upon an inevitable evil, as upon the victims of the social climate, and I preferred to keep my distance from them.' In these words of his, as sincere as any he wrote, there is an echo of certain *motifs* which are also common to Pushkin's *Aleko*. But in Leontiev's time the cultural background of Russian society had become more complex. The army had a greater aesthetic appeal for him than the *literati* and the professors. He had set out in quest of an aesthetic life, of a happiness discoverable in beauty. But he could find neither of these in the cultured society, in the Russian intelligentsia, which he frequented. Like the English and French romantics he was instinctively driven in search of the exotic. He regarded war first and foremost as an aesthetic phenomenon. 'I was terribly afraid that I might live my life without seeing any major war. But as it happened I was fortunate in seeing both the Crimea and

[24]

a war.' He was courageous and fond of adventure; and he hated dull everyday life, everyday work, relationships and sentiments. His whole life through he was trying to escape from this prosaic life, first of all plunging into Eastern exoticism, and then taking refuge in Mount Athos and the Optina monastery. That accounts for his dislike of domesticity, of his relatives, of his brothers. His mother alone evoked a poetic response in him. 'At that time I began to believe that the poet, the artist and the thinker, *should not have* any brothers, sisters or relatives. . . . It was not until I had reached the age of forty and had experienced the crisis, which brought me back to *positive* religion, that I could summon up the strength to remember that an attachment to one's nearest of kin is a more essentially Christian thing than any freely willed friendship with strangers. . . . Alas! my education was not strictly Christian.' But Leontiev was never able to master his instincts. Speaking of Kudinovo, he said: 'where the garden alleys seem so long and mysterious, where the whispering trees say so much more to me than elsewhere, there I discovered something essentially *poetic*.' He felt this poetic element in his mother, in his hunchback aunt and nurse, but not in his brothers. Nor could Leontiev have accepted or liked the everyday prosaic aspects of war; he delighted in it only from afar, in its poetic and aesthetic aspects, in those which were removed from the common round of everyday life among relatives and *literati* in the hot-house atmosphere of modern civilization. His contact with war was but superficial, and he gathered from it some colourful aesthetic experiences.

But he soon grew tired of his doctor's life in the Crimea. His literary ambitions began to manifest themselves. He decided that he had a writer's vocation. He spent his six months' furlough on the estate of a Crimean landowner, Shatilov; and there he started his long novel, *Podlypki*. In 1857 his term of service ended, and he returned to Moscow where he had to set about at once looking for a job. He finally got the post of private doctor to the Baroness Rosen on her Nizhny-Novgorod estate. He stayed there for two years, leading a quiet and pleasant life. But there, too, he was unable to resist the longing for another, richer and more varied life. His position as a country doctor became unbearable to him. He finally decided to give up his medical career and to go back to Kudinovo. He did not, however, stay there very long. He was drawn to Petersburg, the centre of intellectual life. He made up his mind to devote himself entirely to literature and to live by his literary labours.

VI

Petersburg was to disappoint that fine hope. It held in store for Leontiev all kinds of disillusions. He found it hard to make ends meet by literary activity. He was obliged to supplement his meagre income by giving lessons and doing translation work—a dull and painful occupation for a man like him. Leontiev would have liked to be influential and to propagate his ideas in the capital; but his ideas and sentiments were not in harmony with the fashionable ideologies of the day; he did not fit in with the age, and his aestheticism isolated him from his contemporaries. The men of 1860 were complete strangers to the cult of beauty, just as Leontiev was a stranger to the liberal and democratic ideas of the time. In 1862 he broke definitively with these equalitarian ideas, and became a staunch conservative. He has himself given us a vivid description of the incident. One day he was out strolling with a certain Piotrevsky, a contributor to the *Sovremenik* (*The Contemporary*), and a disciple of Tchernishevsky and Dobroliubov. They were walking down the *Nevsky Prospect* and were approaching the *Anitchkov Bridge*, when Leontiev asked Piotrevsky: 'Would you like all men to live in the same kind of house, every one of them comfortable and clean?' To this Piotrevsky replied: 'But of course, what could be better?' Leontiev then retorted: 'In that case, I am from this day no longer one of you. If the consequences of democracy are so horribly prosaic, then I can have no more sympathy with democratic ideas! Until this moment I had no clear conception of what the partisans of progress and revolution were aiming at. . . .'

'While I was speaking,' Leontiev goes on to say, 'we were on the point of traversing the *Anitchkov Bridge*, or at least we were not far off. On our left we could see the rose-coloured Bielosselsky palace, with its stately windows and caryatides; in the background, further along the Fontanka quayside, there was the silhouette of the Troistsky monastery, its church surmounted by a gilded cupola; on our right, giving on the Fontanka canal, were the fishermen's quarters, little yellow houses, and fishermen standing about in their red shirts. I pointed out these sights to Piotrevsky, saying: "That is a living illustration of my thesis. The style of the monastery is Byzantine—it is the style of the Church, of religion; the Bielosselsky palace is rococo—that is the style of the nobility, of the aristocracy; the little yellow houses, the red shirts—that is a picture of the life of the common people. They are all fine and necessary! But you would destroy all this, and in its place you would have nothing but

[27]

little houses as alike as two peas, or six-storey barracks like those on the *Nevsky* Prospect!"—"How fond you are of images!" exclaimed Piotrevsky.—"The images of life" I replied, "are not meant solely for the spectator's pleasure; they are the expression of a supreme inner law—a law that, like all natural laws, cannot be transgressed with impunity."'

It is interesting to note that Leontiev's political sympathies were shaped less by abstract thought or moral experience than by his plastic or pictorial impressions. He became a conservative because he seemed to find more beauty in the Church, the Monarchy, the Army, and the nobility, than in the practices of equality and the life of the middle class. The very image of beauty was for him inseparable from diversity. Beauty was the prerogative of a society founded on variety, inequality and dissimilarity. The criterion of beauty was, indeed, the axiom of Leontiev's social philosophy. He regarded beauty in the light of a vital principle underlying all things. He arrived at this conception as a result of a crisis which was as painful as it was stormy. In the course of it he made a clean sweep of his youthful predilections, of George Sand, of Turgeniev, of the Western European writers, and of all humanitarian notions. As he said himself, 'there were personal elements in this crisis; chance and sentiment played their part independently of purely political or intellectual influences. Yes, I reformed quickly, but in 1860 my mind was given over to so desperate a struggle that I grew quite thin; I spent sleepless nights sitting up with my head in my hands, plunged in painful meditation. I had every respect for ideas, and it was not without anguish that I gave up all that Russian and foreign writers had taught me to worship.' In

[28]

describing his political crisis, just as he was later to describe his religious crisis, Leontiev speaks of the impulses of the heart. And indeed, there were in him certain elements of the inner life, those connected with his relations with women, which were part of his amorous nature and which he never altogether openly revealed.

Thus we may observe the growth in him of an attitude which in many ways anticipated that of Nietzsche, and which has been defined as one of 'aesthetic amoralism'. The first glimpse we have of it is in his novel, *In the Country*. It is there personified by his hero, the scintillating Milneyev, who gives vent to statements such as :'Suffering is indispensable, and so is struggle. . . . I am myself ready to suffer, I have suffered, and I shall suffer. . . . Nor is my reason committed to pity others. As for the ideals of equality, labour, and universal repose, may the Lord preserve us from them!' 'Nature is a sound teacher: nature exults in the variety and infinite wealth of forms; our lives should follow her example, they should be complex and rich. The personality is the essential element of diversity; it is superior to its works. . . . The multiple force of the personality, its quality exalted to its highest pitch—such is the most clearly discernible goal of history. There will be no lack of works as long as there are true men. Which should we prefer: an age like that of the Renaissance, violent but at the same time spiritually magnificent? Or a state of peace, prosperity and moderation such as we find in modern Denmark, Holland, and Switzerland? Beauty is the unique goal of life. Neither morality nor renouncement has any value except as a manifestation of beauty, the free genesis of Good. The higher man's development, the more he believes in beauty and the less use he has for utility.' 'It matters little that the law should be observed or that suffering should be avoided; the essential is that suffering should be noble, that the norm should be left behind—not through weakness or corruption, but in order to obey all the exigencies of passion. Creon and Sophocles were right to condemn Antigone to death. In doing so they represented the law. But Antigone buried her brother because she loved him. And she was also right. Morality is but a minute particle of beauty. If not, how should we judge Alcibiades, a diamond, a tiger?' 'And how do you justify violence?' To this question Milneyev replies: 'By beauty, which is the only criterion of all things.' 'Why should we fear struggle and evil?' he exclaims again. . . . 'Poetry alone is great, for in it both good and evil hold sway. Let good and evil have their winged way, give them room. . . . Open wide the doors. . . . Take and create; be free and daring. . . . If anyone fall on the threshold, destiny is to blame; and what does it matter if it be you or I? . . . That is the most urgent need, that is the substance of all great ages. If Lady Macbeth is necessary for the existence of Cordelia, then long live Lady Macbeth. But spare us impotence, sleep, indifference, vulgarity, a shop-keeper's prudence. . . . Blood is not incompatible with heavenly goodness. . . . Jeanne d'Arc spilled blood, and was she not sweeter than an angel? And what sort of goodness is that which only moans? . . . One ancient oak is worth more than twenty mediocre men, and I would not fell it in order to buy medicaments to cure a few peasants of cholera.'

These words must have sounded strangely in the Russia of 1860, which was so penetrated with humanitarian, liberal and democratic tendencies. To the leaders of that generation such sentiments must have appeared as belonging to quite another world. Their message fell on deaf ears. It began to be appreciated only at the beginning of the twentieth century when we learned to read Nietzsche, Ibsen and the French aesthetes. Leontiev's deeper instincts, his conception of beauty, his revolt against utilitarianism, estranged him from the liberal camp. But solitary contemplation did not appeal to him. He was looking for an aesthetic principle in life much more than in art. And he became a conservative because he believed that the glory of past centuries was based upon this conception of an aesthetic life. The conservatives did not insist upon their supporters doing work of public utility or of general well-being. They left a margin for beauty. And they attracted Leontiev for that reason. But the conservative attitude was very unpopular in the eyes of Russian society. It was even regarded with suspicion on moral grounds. Leontiev had to hold his own against a general wave of disapproval: 'The aesthete *must* be on the side of movement when everything else is motionless; on the side of authority, when license reigns; the artist must be a liberal in a slave state, and an aristocrat when confronted with demagogy; he must be a bit of a freethinker—however little—when opposed to bigotry and hypocrisy; and he should show himself a pious man when face to face with impiety . . . that is to say, he must never bow his head or spirit before the mob.' Leontiev elaborated his conception of the world in an atmosphere of demagogy. He was an aristocrat. In an atmosphere of 'impiety' he became pious. Thus he fulfilled his vocation of the aesthete and artist.

Leontiev had great artistic gifts. These gifts never reached their full development, for his religious crisis put an end to his artistic strivings. The novels which he wrote during the early period of his life were not among his best works. There are fine passages here and there, but even so they are uneven. There is lack of artistic completeness in them. Leontiev was an impressionist before his time. If we think of the age in which he lived, his style and manner strike us as new and original. He had escaped the taint of vulgarity, in the strict sense. He had no social axe to grind. He evinced great daring of thought. As an artist he was evidently preoccupied with erotism, but then, again, there was nothing characteristically Russian in that excess. And he was himself to condemn this aspect of his work later from the standpoint of asceticism. He had a masterly way of conveying sentiments full of languor and beauty evoked by the past. In Leontiev's earlier works there is an echo of Turgeniev. Later his composition acquired greater force and penetration. He was both romantic and realist, and had a great wealth of imagery. The textbooks of Russian literature ignored him completely—a proof of the degree of consciousness of our culture and our lack of aesthetic taste. As an artist Leontiev held himself aloof from the main currents of literature. One might almost say that he was not a Russian writer. But one day he will not fail to be appreciated as a type of pure artist. He loved beauty and hated ugliness. He was an extremely rare phenomenon in the history of Russian literature.

In 1861 Leontiev suddenly departed for Theodosia. There he married Elizaveta Pavlovna Politova, an uncultured little *bourgeoise*, with whom he had already had a liaison during his stay in the Crimea. He did not inform his family of the marriage. He was in love with her, but it would appear not very deeply. He apparently regarded it as his duty to marry this woman, who was not, besides, physically unattractive to him. His predilection went out to simple and naïve girls rather than to young women of cultured society. At first sight, this marriage might appear to be a ridiculous and disastrous incident in Leontiev's life. He was destined, indeed, to suffer its consequences throughout his life. But such unions are never entirely a matter of chance; they have a deep and mysterious significance. It was destiny that confronted Leontiev with this lovely Greek girl whom he was to make his wife; she was primitive and uncultured, good but insignificant; she did not understand him and there was no spiritual communion between them. Nor was it by chance that she finally went mad, and that Leontiev was obliged to live with a mentally infirm person. The very nature of his love was such that it drove him to a like destiny. He regarded his wife's madness as a punishment of his own sins. He had considered family life to be 'terribly prosaic', a sort of 'penal servitude, if it were not embellished by an icon, household gods or the verses of the Koran'.

After the marriage his lack of material means made itself more than ever felt. He attempted to settle down in Kudinovo. But life there was difficult enough. He was assailed with discouragement and despair. At last he resolved to make a position for himself. He chose a diplomatic career. Thanks to the good offices of a friend of his brother's, a certain Stremaoukhov, an official of the Eastern department, he succeeded in getting into one of the departments of the Foreign Office. After a nine months' probation there, he was appointed secretary to the Russian Consulate in Crete. He went out with his wife to Crete in 1865. And there, in the

East, began a new period of his life—without doubt the most brilliant he was to know as a writer. There he found that aesthetic principle of life for which he had been looking in vain elsewhere. But there he was also destined to experience the religious crisis which was to place his life under the sign of Salvation.

CHAPTER II

CONSULAR SERVICE IN THE EAST. THE EX-
OTIC EAST AND THE BOURGEOIS WEST.
STORIES OF CHRISTIAN LIFE IN TURKEY.
'THE EGYPTIAN DOVE.' THE GRECO-BUL-
GARIAN QUESTION. THE RELIGIOUS CRI-
SIS. MOUNT ATHOS. THE RETURN TO
RUSSIA

I

Leontiev's gifted nature developed to its full while he
was a consular officer in the Near East. He felt intoxi-
cated by a new sense of life, by the realization of that happiness through beauty which he had been striving vainly to
capture in Russia. He had fled to the East in order to escape
from the European bourgeois civilization with which
Russia was becoming increasingly contaminated. For the
same reason, Englishmen had sought refuge in Italy, and
Frenchmen had gone to live among primitive tribes or in
the Far East. A romantic wanderlust beckoned men to far
lands where they might forget the squalor of everyday life
in the anaemic and pragmatic West, where they might still
find exotic and picturesque customs. In this way a new
awareness of our own mode of life as well as that of exotic
peoples was gained. Our daily existence tends to become intolerably prosaic—a mere struggle for life and an expression
of immediate necessity; but we see the life of other peoples,

of the Oriental races especially, in a poetic light because we are not bound to them by material ties or boring relationships. This feeling is shared by Chateaubriand and Stendhal, Gauguin and Paul Claudel, the Pre-Raphaelites and Walter Pater. This strain of romantic escapism was also deeply engrained in Leontiev. He preached what he believed in—the aspiration for and faith in an original Russian culture. He was never tired of stressing the beauty and singularity of Russian life when compared with that of Western Europe, distorted by its bourgeois civilization. But that was only one of Leontiev's many illusions. When he was in Russia he suffered almost invariably from fits of insatiable melancholy. There is nothing to show that he enjoyed Russian life on the aesthetic plane. More often than not he inveighed against its mediocrity and hideousness, experiencing an eternal dissatisfaction and a yearning to see other countries. Unlike the Slavophils, he was in no sense tradition-bound. He had been uprooted from his ancestral soil. An aesthete is not usually a traditionalist. It was in the East, in Greece and Turkey—that is to say, from afar—that Leontiev appreciated the beauty and originality of Russian life, of a cultural Russian type, and elaborated his doctrine of an original national culture. In the same way Tyutchev laid the foundations of his Slavophilism in Rome. Thus the wealth and diversity of Leontiev's life in the East was only an escape, a break with the dull life he had lived in Russia.

Leontiev was a man of complex culture. His disgust with modern civilization, his struggle against it, his manner of idealizing ancient customs and primitive force, were all signs of a cultivated mind in love with a culture at once splendid and diverse. Leontiev gave faithful expression to this awareness which exalted the image of Beauty above blood and race; his consciousness was, indeed, an uprooted one. Hence his destiny was a tragic one. For none of the leading Slavophils like Kireyevsky, Khomyakov or Aksakov, had ever turned to the East in search of the diverse and the complex, of the beauty implicit in perfect form.

The Slavophils had no conception of the schism accompanying the birth of a new soul. Those of the older type, which is still to be met with to-day, would not have concurred with Leontiev when he said: 'I am infinitely fond of this consular service which bears no resemblance to the ordinary official routine pursued at home. A consul's activity is almost free from modern European, bourgeois and progressive elements; it offers vast scope for freedom, for personal discrimination between good and evil . . . so much room for independence and inspiration . . . provincial life in Turkey is at the same time both pastoral and feudal.' These words were spoken by the hero of Leontiev's charming story, *The Egyptian Dove*. But Leontiev is here obviously dealing with *his own life*, and the sentiments are his. *The Egyptian Dove* was an expression of a purely pagan joy in life and beauty. In the epilogue are set down the words of a man who has forever lost his faith in life, in the possibility of terrestrial joy, in the survival of beauty upon earth, but who is still capable of evoking it: 'I had started to write in a moment of overflowing joy, when I still dared to think that the canticle of life was not yet at an end. Whilst my poor dove was cooing perched on a branch of a pear-tree, I gave myself up to yearnings, I had such a deep passion for life. . . . Even sufferings brought me sometimes infinite pleasure.' 'I believed then, that I had a right to earthly happiness, to the ideal joys of life.' He lived those brief moments most intensely: 'How I am happy, O my God! I feel such lightness and such sweet warmth, wrapped in my Russian mantle of blue cloth! I am so glad to be a Russian! And so happy to be still young! And happy too, to be living in Turkey! The dear, dear smoke, the grey smoke of domestic work! How you rise, friendly and hospitable, over the roofs of the populous and peaceful town! Strolling along the bank of the river from Makhel-Nepru, the sunset grows ever more purple and splendid. I gaze at the horizon, I sigh, I am happy. . . . And how should I not be? Along the river bank, on that charming road which I love so much, and which stretches from Makhel-Nepru to the town gates, there are mulberry-trees in bloom. In that enchanting nook along the river bank—enchanting for *me*, for *my heart* brimming with joy—I catch sight of three little faded leaves, white on one side, and black and velvety on the other; and on the black velvet background there are silver flaws, stars of wintry beauty! . . . I am happy, I suffer, I am madly in love with this life, I love all the passers-by on the road; I love that Bulgarian with the grey moustache and blue turban, who has just greeted me with a deep bow; I am in love with that tall slender Turk with frowning mien who walks ahead of me in his red fez. I should like to embrace them both, I love them equally well!'

This passage gives us an idea of the exalted atmosphere, of the aesthetic ecstasy, of Leontiev's life in the Balkans. How little there is in common between his experiences and those of Moscow, Petersbourg and the Russian countryside! . . . He was living a full life, 'fulfilling his duty towards life's plenitude'. He knew how to adorn life with poetry and beauty even to excess. It was in this period of Leontiev's life that Rozanov discovered an Alcibiadian element in him: 'After his death, on looking through *that monk's* library, I came across a thick volume entitled *Alcibiades*—a French monograph on the great Athenian. I have found nowhere except in Leontiev such a revival of the Athenian principle, of the riotous *Agora*, of the passionate strife of parties, and of that 'familiarity with gods as with men', peculiar to Greece. All the Fillalières and the Petrarchs are but doll-like imitators of the Greeks in comparison with this Kaluga landowner who imitated no-one, who was an incarnation of Alcibiades returned from the confines of Asia, escaping from arrows and flying from the burning house of his mistress.' Rozanov further discerned in Leontiev a 'wild and leonine' quality, and he coined such phrases for him as 'a man of the wilderness', 'an unbridled horse'. He says of him moveover: 'Leontiev was the first Russian—perhaps the first European—who discovered the pathos of "Turkishness", that of a warlike soul susceptible to women, full of religious naïveté and fanaticism, of faith in God and of singular degrees of respect for man. "A Turkish monk!" I could not help saying, after re-reading his account of the conversation between a mullah and a young Turk who was in love with a Christian woman.'

Rozanov failed to grasp the whole spiritual complexity of Leontiev as well as of his religious vocation. He was not interested in discovering the Christian in Leontiev. But then, at the end of the 1860's and at the beginning of the 1870's, Leontiev was indeed much as Rozanov had described him. He was in love with the Turks and Islam; and the love he bore them was to act later as a sort of vaccine. It was destined to exercise an influence upon his Christianity and, for this very reason, to deform it.

II

Leontiev started his consular career in Crete. The island enchanted him. 'The six months I spent in Crete', he wrote 'were like a honeymoon in my consular career; I strolled by the seashore, I dreamt in the shade of olive trees, I got to know the inhabitants of that island, so full of poetry, I went for walks in the mountains.' He dedicated to Crete his exquisite stories, *Sketches of Crete, Krozo, Chamad and Makaly*. However, he stayed only six months in Crete. He was obliged to leave the island because he struck the French Consul with a whip for having spoken slightingly of Russia. He was recalled to Adrianople, where, at the end of four months, he was appointed Consular Secretary. In the Consul's absence he was left virtually in charge of the Consulate. His new place of residence did not please him overmuch, and he was bored by the bourgeois society of the town. Moreover, as he was short of money, he got into debt. His salary was quite inadequate to satisfy his expensive tastes. He thought that his position as secretary was not in keeping with his age. Invited to various town festivals, he danced to the sound of Turkish music with the pretty young girls of Adrianople. He was also fond of organizing wrestling matches. In 1867 he was transferred to Tulcha. There he led an easier and more agreeable life. 'I have but one wish,' he wrote to K. A. Gubastov, 'and that is to settle down in Tulcha. . . . There one finds both peace and excitement. It is both the East and the West, the North and the South.' He was in the good graces of Count Ignatiev, the Russian ambassador at Constantinople. Everything appeared to be going well with him, when of a sudden his wife exhibited the first signs of insanity. Everything points to jealousy as being the direct cause of her insanity. His wife had been suffering from his repeated infidelities. Her illness was to prove the great trial of Leontiev's life.

In 1869 he was appointed Consul at Janina. There he contracted malaria. In 1871 he was Consul at Salonika. Thus his advancement in the service had been rapid and brilliant. During this period Leontiev's pagan cult of love and voluptuousness had attained its highest expression. He had many amorous adventures. His erotic fancy would permit of no barriers; he loved his wife, but he was persistently unfaithful to her. The daughters of the Near East were a source of endless temptation to him. Writing to his colleague Gubastov, Leontiev gives him the following advice: 'To get to know thoroughly the poetry of Adrianople, you should: (1) take a mistress at once, a naïve Bulgarian or Greek girl; (2) go as often as you can to the Turkish bath; (3) Try and get hold of a Turkish woman, it is not very difficult; (4) do not let yourself be flattered by the attention of the Franks and do not over-praise Madame Badetti; (5) go for frequent walks along the banks of the Tundja and think of me; (6) make an appointment one day with a Kavas in the Mosque of the Sultan Bajazet, and on the lawn there, near the kiosque, organize a wrestling match between young Turks to the beating of a drum. It's fine!'

We may conjecture that Leontiev himself carried out that programme. He did know Bulgarian, Greek and Turkish women. In another passage to Gubastov he said: 'Do not imagine that my life is colourless; alas, it is very stormy! You ask me why I am always preoccupied with suffering humanity (that is to say, the Cretans), and not with myself? In the first place I am concerned much less with suffering humanity than with poetic humanity; and in the second, my own person is in no wise neglected.' In the same letter he mentioned his wife's illness. After saying that she had lost her good looks, he added: 'I have affairs of the heart and what affairs!' Leontiev made a distinction between love on the one hand, and marriage and family on the other: 'Marriage is a division of labour, a heavy responsibility—inevitable and holy, but nevertheless heavy, which society forces upon us like taxes, work, war, and so on. Both work and war have their pleasant moments and their poetry, one can admire them, but we must admit that the one is generally extremely trying and the other is very hard and perilous. Why are people unwilling to regard marriage as a social servitude—one that is not lacking in poetry either but one which can be distinguishable from war and work in that war, for all its peril, is never trying, and that work is trying without being dangerous. Now marriage is physically dangerous for women and in general most trying for men. I subscribe to the opinion of the Frenchman who said: *L'amour n'a rien à faire avec les devoirs pénibles et sévères du mariage.*' I do not understand how one can be jealous of one's legitimate wife. It is far too primitive!' Leontiev did not feel that need to work which is one of life's dictates. He was too much of a gentleman to be visibly affected by it. Work and the burden of marriage and family ran counter to his aestheticism; the romantic in him rebelled against anything prosaic or commonplace. Later on, when this romanticism gave way to monastic asceticism, he wrote: '*Romantic and moral idealism*

[42]

as well as Christian spirituality are quite different things. Marriage is a spiritual sacrament, and not a realization of an ideal of the heart; this latter may easily deceive us. But for a believer a sacrament is always a sacrament. A believer is not likely to forget that fact even if the marriage turns out to be an unhappy one.'

Leontiev was naturally inclined to polygamy. He saw no reasonable argument in favour of the Christian marriage. In that respect he was a Turk; and his libertinism made him sympathize with Islam rather than with Christianity. In the Christian ideal he saw a challenge to his own nature, a sort of distraint on his person. 'It is only with the help of Christian dogma, of Christian Faith, that one can refute polygamy; but if reason is the only guide, then one can go as far as preaching polyandry. . . . If we dispense with positive religion, then the only thing we have left is *artistic sentiment.* There is every occasion to feel some apprehension; we have to admit to our shame that we prefer the Sultan of Turkey to the "honest" European atheist or even deist who (one does not know how or why!) lives quietly with his rational wife—not for *the glory of God* but for that of *reason.*' In this respect Leontiev differed from the Slavophils who were extremely virtuous men and who upheld the ideal of the family.

The lack of romanticism in the Orthodox East was a source of displeasure to Leontiev. 'I knew perfectly well what I disliked in the East . . . it was the rigid attitude of our fellow Christians towards love. I hated their lack of romanticism where the life of the heart was involved—of that romanticism to which I had become accustomed during my childhood in Russia. In that sense alone I was a "European" to the bitter end. I adored all the nuances of romanticism starting with its purest, most ascetic form, and ending with the noble and refined cult of the flesh which is so finely expressed in the poems of Goethe, Pushkin, Alfred de Musset and Fet.' The Christians of the East seemed to be impervious to the passionate song of love: 'There exists another aspect of life which is intimately related to the question of romanticism—that is the *family*. . . . Everyone knows how contradictory are the relations between the Christian family and the romanticism of the heart but yet deep-rooted and inalterable. Sometimes we see the cult of tenderness and the spiritualism of Christian abstinence (a trifle dry perhaps) merge, and complete themselves in the spacious and varied life of really civilized societies—raising the ideal of family to its highest degree of purity, elegance and poetry. At other times, on the contrary, we see them opposed to one another in a desperate and tragic struggle. These two principles have from time immemorial been active in the history of Western society and their influence is deeply rooted even in the unconscious mind. They have been able to arrive at a perfect harmony under the auspices of the Church. But at times they have given rise to those conflicts with which we are painfully familiar, and to which the drama, poetry, the novel, music, and painting, owe so many noble and inspired moments. I have failed to discover anything comparable to this in the East among Christians of the cultivated classes.'

The hero of Leontiev's *The Egyptian Dove* was made the mouthpiece of these romantic thoughts and sentiments. As he said himself, he became a European by the very fact of championing 'the cult of tender passions'. This romanticism was not only alien to the Christians of the East, but also to the Russians whose literature bears almost no trace of the cult of love. In this respect Leontiev was much more of a European than might appear, much more of a European than he himself realized. He was in love with the old, chivalrous, Catholic and romantic Europe. He hated only modern bourgeois and democratic Europe, which he accused of having betrayed its ancient beauty. 'Christianity does not deny the illusory and tortuous beauty of Evil; it is satisfied with teaching us to struggle against it, and it sends to our help the Angel of Prayer and of Renunciation. That is why the confusion of amorous and religious romanticism is so dangerous for our soul.'

Only a European, an Occidental, could have expressed himself in this way. We also are indebted to Leontiev for an aphorism on our black dress clothes. He compared this garment to 'a paltry mourning suit which the West has donned as a sign of mourning for its glorious past, its religious, aristocratic and artistic past'. It is evident that only a man who was passionately aware of the ancient glory of the West could have been capable of such intense hatred for Europe's suits of solemn black. This is extremely significant for our understanding of Leontiev's outlook on the world. The essential principles of his mind were fundamentally different from those of the Slavophils, and his theory had only a very superficial connection with their doctrine. There was, on the other hand, an affinity between him and Chaadayev—an affinity noted by Leontiev's friend, Gubastov.

III

Leontiev's life in the East proved to be a first class stimulus for his literary work. His most important works were written under the influence of the feelings and thoughts excited by his sojourn there. Those exotic countries helped him to formulate definitively his spiritual personality, to sharpen his political, philosophical and religious outlook, and finally to develop his talent as a writer. He used this newly acquired power almost exclusively to describe the life of Christians in Turkey. Leontiev's literary output would have been very different had he not been a consul in the Balkans. His pages are sprinkled with Oriental imagery. He found it almost impossible to escape from his Oriental theme, which gave an added farce to his meditations and embraced the whole world. His Oriental imagery was intimately related to beauty and the joy of life. The consequence of this was a certain narrowness, a monotony even, a lack of variety in his work. In the East he endeavoured to realize not only an aesthetic of art but also of life. He was incapable of devoting himself exclusively to the arts as did the French aesthetes. Nor could he content himself with abstract philosophical contemplation. He felt the need of a stirring life crowded with images of plastic beauty. His aestheticism excluded any compromise with the mean. He was particularly fond of Constantinople. It satisfied his aesthetic sense more fully than any other place. 'I love the life itself in that Embassy (Constantinople),' he wrote to Gubastov. 'I love its occupations and interests; there are few members of that circle whom I fail to recall with pleasure, sympathy and gratitude. I love that town, the Islands, the Greeks and the Turks. . . . I love everything there, and you may be certain that I feel keenly the fact that I am unable to settle down there forever. Neither Moscow, Petersbourg, nor Kudinovo, neither the most lucrative posts nor the saintliest of monas-

teries, could afford me as much satisfaction as Constantinople. . . . Alone the life of Constantinople (where hermits
are still to be found in the forests of the island of Khalki,
where the Ignatievs hold their receptions, where the politics
are alive and the *mass is most solemn*, and where there is an
infinite variety of literary subjects) . . . that multiple life
alone can satisfy my *intolerably* refined tastes.'

Leontiev's longing for Constantinople was to haunt him
his whole life through. His deepest aspirations were bound
up with that city. And it is difficult to say which of its aspects
—the Turkish or the Byzantine—was dearer to him. He
regarded Greece and Constantinople in the same light as
other writers regarded Italy and Rome. He was conscious of
the beauty of ancient Europe, but he was not directly in
contact with it; he did not draw his inspiration from it, for
he was too disgusted with modern bourgeois Europe. All
his hopes of a 'complex and flourishing culture' were centred
in the East. He attached an enormous importance to the
style and the plastic side of life. He believed that modern
European dress—the jacket and dress suit—exercised a fatal
influence on the soul of Europeans. This dress was a symbol
to him of corruption and death. In the East the corruption
was not so widespread, although Leontiev had already discovered threatening symptoms and had foretold their
consequences.

'All true artists, poets, thinkers, gifted with an aesthetic
sense, have little love for the *average man*.' In 'their *heart of
hearts* they love the nobility, high society, the court, military
deeds'. 'Byron fled from the *civilized* countries in order to
live among the *wild and forsaken* gardens of Italy, Spain, and
Turkey. At that time Ali Pascha was still living in Janina, and

his ferocity was more picturesque than the commonplace savagery of the French communards. Italy was still the enchanted kingdom of ruins and ivy, of Calabrian brigands, Madonnas and monks. The "constitutional " King of Sardinia had not yet locked the Patriarch of Rome in the prison of the Vatican. Nor had he with the help of the defenders of progress as yet transformed the Eternal City into the vulgar capital of a mediocre State. In Spain no one blushed as yet at the idea of bull-fighting. The great man who gave his life for Greece could not foresee that the picturesque Greece of the fustanella–clad corsairs was the product of Asiatic oppression, and that as soon as the Turkish yoke had been cast off the corsair would don a cheap jacket and spend his days gossiping in the bars of Athens.' 'How can a living poetry survive without mysticism and religious pomp, without the pageantry and the severities of the State, without a brilliant and firmly established nobility? . . . Will it not become the poetry of *happiness for all*, that of *rational bourgeois contentment?*' . . . Thus, Leontiev was concerned less with 'reflected aestheticism with what is depicted in paintings or in books, than with the aestheticism of life itself. He believed, and still hoped, that the aestheticism of life, that of *unity in complexity*, would survive in the East. For Western man it was irremediably lost, for him even 'reflected aestheticism' had become impossible. But Leontiev was forced to admit that exoticism and picturesqueness were also beginning to die out in the East. This decease was particularly noticeable among the Balkan Slavs. He had no liking for these latter, and saw no cause to have any hope in them. As we shall see later, he believed in the Byzantine spirit, in Greek Orthodoxy, and in Turkey, as the bulwark

[48]

standing in the way of liberal and equalitarian progress, and of general corruption. As a result of his observation of the life of the Slavs in Turkey and the Balkans, Leontiev lost faith in the principles of race and nationality. From then on, he began to adopt a negative attitude towards Panslavism. Later, he was to give vent to profound and trenchant ideas on the subject of nationalist policies.

Leontiev's inner drama, which was to lead to his religious crisis with its mystical terrors and urge towards Salvation, had its origin in his passion for life, his taste for enchantment and earthly beauty, and the sense of their fleeting and fugitive nature. This sense of death and of the perishable nature of all earthly things had haunted Leontiev long before his conversion. It was an inherent part of his romantic temperament —of that romantic character which, in the name of Beauty, was the prey of contradictions, sufferings and unrealizable desires. The coexistence of good and evil was one of the tenets of his aesthetic doctrine, and that was not without its influence upon his Christianity.

In this spiritual atmosphere Leontiev's artistic nature ripened and matured. He wrote some admirable stories about the life of Greeks under Turkish rule, and their merit has yet to be fully appreciated. Some of them are characterized by an extraordinary degree of objectivity, especially in the descriptions of oriental ways of life. We may note in particular the stories included in the second volume of his collected works, such as *Sketches of Crete, Chrizo*, and so on. The legend entitled *Child of the Soul* is equally successful. At the same time, he wrote purely personal works—*The Egyptian Dove* is the best of these—in which he was exclusively concerned with his own destiny. This work is of great autobiographical value. The narrator of the story is a diplomat, like Leontiev himself, who has set out to find happiness through beauty, and a thrilling life in the East. For the most part the story is characterized by a peculiarly pagan joy and voluptuousness, by a very personal erotism. But his hero is relating his history after an inner catastrophe has overwhelmed him and made him lose all hope in earthly happiness. One day he finds himself betrayed by all earthly things, even by the most beautiful and radiant manifestations. But on entering a church, at the moment when the deacon is speaking, invoking 'a peaceful and painless death', and imploring God's mercy at the Last Judgment, 'he experiences the sudden impulse to prostrate himself.' He remains thus, beating his forehead on the ground and thinking: 'But of course it is that, and that alone, I must wish for myself.' And forthwith the image of the woman he loved seems to fade away.

The Egyptian Dove is a retrospective vision, rich in themes taken from Leontiev's reminiscences. It mirrors the years he spent in the consular service, all the fickle and illusory joys of that period of his life.

A Husband's Confession (*Ai Bouroun*) is one of Leontiev's best literary works. He condemned this work later, and forbade its re-publication. He castigated it in the following terms: 'This work is in the highest degree immoral, sensual, pagan and diabolical; it is the height of perversion. There is certainly nothing Christian in its pages, but they are written with talent and daring, with all the sincerity of a deeply perverted heart. . . . I hope they will not be printed *as* they *are*. . . . It would be a sin, a great sin, for they are well written and have plenty of talent.'

There is something painful in Leontiev's judgment of his own work, something reminiscent of Gogol's or Botticelli's drama.

A Husband's Confession is an extremely subtle work, and its spirit is quite new; it is a unique work of its kind in Russian literature. It depicts the erotic nature of an infinitely complex soul, one that has little in common with that of the men of 1860. The hero of this work is a middle-aged man who is in love with a young girl; but he renounces her and at the same time encourages her to fall in love with a rival. The writing is the acme of elegance such as was rare at the time in Russia. In Leontiev's opinion his best work was the long novel he devoted to Greek ways of life, *Polychroniades Odyssey*. I do not feel obliged, however, to agree with Leontiev. The work has many excellent passages which bear witness to a profound understanding of the Greek soul, but it is lengthy to the point of tediousness. Leontiev was not made to write works of great scope; his temperament was that of an impressionist. His shorter stories were his best, even when he attempts the epic and ethnological genre. He put in a lot of work on a cycle of novels entitled, *The River of Times*. It was to form a sort of fresco of events drawn from Russian life between 1811 and 1862. Perhaps Leontiev's talent would have found therein a definitive expression. But this work was never to see the light of day, as we shall learn hereafter. Leontiev's artistic gifts were more powerful than original. There is every indication that, had he devoted himself whole-heartedly to literature, he would have made a name for himself. But he was incapable of creating anything in any domain except that of his own life. And in this respect his destiny was typically Russian. For in spite of many western traits, Leontiev followed the vocation of a Russian writer in quest of life and Salvation.

IV

The Eastern question was Leontiev's chief political interest —the very kernel of his social and historical philosophy. His approach to this very involved question was quite original, differing essentially from that of the Slavophils and the Conservatives.

The Greeks and the Turks were his favourite Balkan peoples; he had hardly any sympathy for the Slavs. He detested the Bulgarians most of all. Whenever any conflict arose he invariably sided with the Greeks or Turks against the Slavs, whose democratic tendencies alienated him. He feared the triumph of Western liberal equalitarian ideas in the Southern Slav world, the victory in the near future of the levelling Western bourgeois principle. He noted that the Southern Slavs lacked those strong traditions which alone had any chance of impeding the fatal process of decay. His aristocratic distaste for Slav democracy was in no wise a Russian trait. On the contrary, it was that which, distinguished him from the Slavophils. His preferences went out to the Poles because they had an aristocratic sense and were faithful to Catholicism. In the East he had a high regard for the Greeks as the guardians of the orthodox Byzantine traditions. The monastic spirit was very strongly rooted in the Greeks. They at least struggled in the name of the principles of the Church against democratic progress. Loyalty to the Byzantine traditions and heritage appeared to Leontiev to be the only serious bastion standing in the way of those universal processes which threatened to engulf the Balkan peoples. Among the Slavs, however, he noted no awareness of these Byzantine principles. On the other hand, the Turks had an aesthetic appeal for him because of their colourful patriarchal ways of life which 'thrilled' him deeply. According to him, the Turkish yoke prevented the Balkan peoples from falling definitively into the abyss of European democratic progress, and helped to preserve the old Orthodoxy in the East. He even regarded the Turkish persecutions of Christians as beneficial from that point of view: 'As long as life was dangerous, as long as the Turks indulged in violence, killed, plundered and burnt, the Christian was more of a man. He went to Church only at night, and was always treated like a dog. . . . He was more of a man! I mean that he was nearer the ideal. In the 'twenties and 'thirties of this century there were still martyrs, there were still mothers who could say to their sons, "I'd rather see you massacred by the Turks than turn renegade." Formerly only the wealthy and the noble entered monasteries. . . . The Church's political success had only helped to weaken mystical and individual Orthodoxy, the Orthodoxy of the heart. Freedom had opened the doors to paltry European ideas, to vulgar Western pride.' Thus Leontiev dissociated himself from the cause of Slav emancipation; for it was Byzantinism rather than Slavism that attracted him in the East. The interests of the Church were paramount in his eyes; political interests were secondary and subordinate to them. In his eyes European democracy and progress was a greater danger to Orthodoxy and the Slav world than the Turkish yoke and Turkish violence. He would rather have seen the Turkish power preserved in the Balkans as a bulwark against the victory of the false liberating principle which he hated with all his soul.

The 'Turk' was an antidote against the *petit bourgeois* poison. A democratic and liberal Slavophilism went against his deeper instincts, and he parted ways with Aksakov on the question of Slav policy in the East. As a result Leontiev came to be regarded by his contemporaries as a traitor to the Slav cause and to Russian political traditions. In reality Leontiev proved to be more perspicacious and far-seeing than his detractors. Many of his prophecies have come true. He had an amazing grasp of the universal principles underlying history, and he was at the mercy neither of external emotions nor of actual politics. He was passionately interested in the Eastern question, because he was concerned above all with the destiny of the Church, that of humanity and, finally, that of Russia and the whole world. But Leontiev was never willing to examine Russian orthodoxy in the light of the truths applicable to the Eastern Slavs. In the same way, it might be argued that the persecutions 'which force the Christian to go to Church only at night' do help to stimulate the zeal of Russian orthodoxy now; and that State protection on the contrary only encourages decadence in the Church; that it is not only Turkish oppression but also Bolshevism which saves Christians from the *petit bourgeois* sins.

In contradistinction to the Slavophils and to Danilevsky, Leontiev denied both the autonomy of the Slav world and the unity of its culture. He believed neither in race nor in nationality. He refused to admit their primacy. According to him nationality should be animated and dominated by a supreme idea. For him this supreme idea was synonymous with Byzantinism. The Eastern Slavs were but indifferent representatives of this idea, and they were certainly not its

[54]

infallible champions. They were too ready to welcome other ideas, and second rate, liberal and democratic truths. Thus Leontiev regarded Panslavism as a danger for Russia and the Russian ideal in the world: 'In the light of a certain original culture which I hold valuable, it was clear to me that all Southern and Western Slavs represented an *inevitable political evil* for us Russians. Until now these peoples have not given anything to the world but a most ordinary and vulgar kind of *modern bourgeoisie*.' Leontiev's distrust of any idea of an Eastern Slav Union, his disgust with Slav democratic trends, was apparent in his cruel passage about the Czechs whom he liked even less than the Balkan Slavs: 'It would be very fortunate if the Germans *compelled* us to allow them to absorb the Czechs, for they are about to join in their turn the great alliance of Eastern Slavs. That would be a real calamity. The Czechs are to a great extent European bourgeois; they are bourgeois and "honest liberals" to the core. Their liberal and pretentious *Burger* spirit is otherwise more dangerous than the turbulence of the Polish nobility; it is a peaceful permeation, an internal *chemical* poison. Their *Hussism* is far more dangerous than Jesuitism. . . . If it were necessary to suffer two defeats at the hands of the Germans in order that circumstances might *oblige* us to give up the Czechs to them, for my part I should wish those two battles lost.' This passage may shock us, but Leontiev wrote it with all the sincerity, radicalism and daring of which he alone knew the secret. He spared neither himself nor others. He invoked German violence against the Czechs just as he invoked Turkish violence against the Balkan Slavs with only one end in view, and that was to prevent the Slav world from becoming bourgeois. In his mind a state of Christian

[55]

slavery was more desirable than state Christian freedom. He believed that oppression would make the Slavs spiritually nobler and more independent. Liberty would only have the effect of suppressing their original character and of making them nonentities. They would exalt democratic principles above those of the Church and above the lofty traditions of the past. Leontiev did not believe for a moment in the immanent forces of the Slav spirit; he saw nothing worthy of attention in it. He preferred the Greeks, the Germans and the Turks. By his sympathies and instinctive tastes he was far more 'anti-slavophil' than the majority of our Westerners, liberals and democrats. Aksakov and the Slavophils protested vigorously against the singular conceptions of this thinker, who adamantly refused to have anything to do with the national movement of the Balkan Slavs. 'At first sight,' he said, 'this Christian movement may appear more *national* than *democratic*. But it is only a *particular form* of the whole process of democratization of which all Europe is at this moment the theatre. . . . If the Turks were driven out of Constantinople, and Russia failed to replace their conservative rule by a discipline of her own, Constantinople would become the centre of an international Revolution which would eclipse that of Paris.' Thus, according to Leontiev, Constantinople should remain in Turkish hands until the day when it would become Russian. He was afraid not only of the collapse of the Ottoman Empire but also of that of the Austrian Empire. 'We must beware lest our triumph be too great, lest we should find ourselves suddenly, and without being ready for it, confronted with millions of new Slav brothers animated by ideas of liberty and equality.'

Leontiev's paradoxical views could not make many converts or exercise any great influence on Slav policy. His 'reactionary' doctrine came before its time; he had looked too far ahead. Later he was to write: 'There was a time, some ten or fifteen years back, when I hoped that my articles would serve "some purpose". . . . Then I believed naïvely that I would "open the eyes of those who mattered". . . . I am constantly being justified by events but not by men's attitude or their critical justice towards me. Now I no longer believe that I can be of any use to anyone; I have enough grounds for thinking that my literary occupation, if not entirely useless, is at any rate well in advance of its time.'

In the religious quarrel which opposed Greece and Bulgaria, Leontiev firmly supported the Greeks, although the Slavophils, Katkov, our ambassador, Count Ignatiev, and Russian opinion as a whole all espoused the cause of Bulgaria. This quarrel originated as follows: in ecclesiastical matters the Bulgarians owed allegiance to the Greek Patriarch of Constantinople; but in their desire for independence they broke away from their spiritual head. In 1872 a Council was convoked in Constantinople and the Bulgarians were declared to be 'schismatics'. Our Slav policy in the East necessitated our showing some signs of sympathy with the Bulgarians in what came to be regarded as a Bulgarian movement of national independence. Leontiev, on the other hand, interpreted the Council's decision as a blow to the unity of the Orthodox Church in the East, a weakening of Patriarchal authority and a victory of democratic over Byzantine principles. Leontiev always placed religious and ecclesiastical interests above those of the State. In his eyes the Orthodox Church in the East was more precious than the Slav world. He referred to the popular Russian attitude in this dispute as a 'Bulgarocraze'. And he was perspicacious enough to see that politically the Bulgarians would never be friends of Russia. That, however, was not the essential point. He was loath to accept the democratization of the Church, a process which the claims of Bulgarian nationalism fatally encouraged. He was the advocate of a strictly hier-archical government of the Church. In his opinion, both Katkov and Aksakov had plunged headlong into the error —into the 'Greco-Bulgarian problem'. 'If there was any difference between the two writers, it was that Aksakov's error was doubtlessly more sincere and naïve than Katkov's. It was an essentially Slav and liberal error like *his very faith*. The same could certainly not be said of Katkov. There was evidence that he had further aims which were, indeed, in-finitely more damaging to the Church. He was apparently seeking to undermine in advance all the Churches of the East, so that, when the moment for solving the Eastern ques-tion came, Russian officials would not find any serious obstacle in their path. . . . That is the spirit of Theophan Prokopovitch and his kidney!' . . . Leontiev detested that patriotic policy whose aim it was to transform and subjugate the Church. Like Vladimir Solovyev he believed that the Church should be set above immediate national policies.

This Greco-Bulgarian question gave rise to a dispute between Leontiev and Count Ignatiev, a dispute so serious that it brought the writer's diplomatic career to an end. Other issues of a more personal nature were also involved. In any case, Leontiev had to resign from the service; he was no adept at compromise. Besides, his exotic Oriental phase was drawing to a natural end. He had just experienced a very severe crisis which was destined to alter the course of his life.

[58]

V

It is impossible to determine the causes, the reasons, and the secret impulses by which a man is brought to the brink of a religious crisis. But once he has gone that far, his inner being lives in a new dimension. He becomes an enigma to his fellow-beings; he incarnates the mystery of a personal, unique and inimitable existence. Nor is he himself able to throw any light on this mystery which has now become part of him. There are several different types of conversion, and we may analyse the motives behind them. But we only arrive at an abstraction which has little in common with the complex reality of the personality. Our hypotheses only lead us to the threshold of the mystery of conversion, but its intimate depths remain a closed book for us.

The causes which produced Leontiev's spiritual upheaval in 1871—an upheaval which proved an illumination for his whole life—are still obscure. He himself alludes only vaguely to the subject. We are quite ready to understand why a man of his stamp should have undergone such a crisis. Moreover, we can distinguish the type of his conversion and we know the external event that set the crisis in motion. But we are quite ignorant of the facts, as well as of the psychological factors, preceding that capital event. From 1869 onwards we can observe various symptoms auguring the drama. Thus, for example, he wrote to Gubastov: 'And above all my heart is haunted by a sadness such as I have never before experienced. It is my inner life which must be held responsible.' Leontiev had known deception, doubt and weariness; the thrill of life had worn off for him. He had become aware of the vanity of attempting to find happiness in beauty.

Every sin has its own inevitable punishment. His soul was already in a turmoil. In 1871 Leontiev was stricken by grave intestinal disease, which he believed to be cholera. The doctor was of no assistance, and Leontiev thought that his last hour had struck. He was haunted by the terrors of death and damnation. Gubastov throws some significant light on this phase: 'He had especially an aesthetic horror of his illness. He often described to me the terror he felt at dying in such a prosaic manner.' Leontiev shut himself in a dark room, so that he might be oblivious of the days and nights. Then of a sudden, at the height of his anguish, a miracle supervened—he was reborn in the spirit. Leontiev has described that moment in a letter addressed to Rozanov. The account is somewhat reticent, especially in the explanation it offers of the phenomenon itself. But it constitutes the only evidence there is.

'There were *a number* of reasons,' he said. 'There were reasons of the *heart* as well as those of the *spirit*, and there were *external reasons* which are usually *attributed to chance*, but in which the supreme theology sometimes manifests itself otherwise than in that inner evolution of which the purpose is accessible to man. I believe nevertheless that we must consider everything thoroughly, and in the first place the philosophical bias of old date (1861–62) against *the spirit of modern European life*. Then there is attachment—an aesthetic and somewhat childish attachment—to the *outer forms* of Orthodoxy. Add to that a sudden and violent shock, a profound upheaval (you know the French proverb, "Cherchez la femme!"). And lastly, an accident, to wit a serious and unexpected illness, and the fear of dying, just as I had conceived but not yet written my *Hypothesis of the Triple Process* and the *Polychroniades Odyssey*. At that time I had not yet expressed my opinion of the "Southern Slavs", nor those condemnations of Europeanism and atheism, which I maintain to be my most valuable contribution on the historical plane. In a word, the essentials of my work are to be found in what I wrote after 1872; that is, after my pilgrimage to Mount Athos, and after my return to personal Orthodoxy. . . . At the age of forty, I do not know quite how, my belief in God put an end to my artistic and political activity. That is always a source of surprise to me. It has always been a mystery and completely incomprehensible. But when, in the summer of 1871, I was in Salonika, stretched out on the divan where I had thrown myself down in the grip of cholera, haunted by the fear of a lightning death, when gazing at the image of the Holy Virgin which a monk from Mount Athos had brought me, I certainly could not yet foresee what was going to happen. Even my literary projects were very vague. I was not then in the least preoccupied with *the salvation of my soul* (for the idea of a personal God was nearer to me than that of *my own immortality*). I believe that I was not a coward, but I was terrified at the thought of my bodily decay. *Prepared already* by a whole series of psychological avatars, of likes and dislikes, I suddenly began to believe in the existence and power of the Holy Virgin; I believed in it so strongly and sincerely that I might have been gazing at a *living and familiar woman*, a very benign and very powerful woman. I cried out, "O Mother of God, it is too soon, it is too soon for me to die! . . . I have done nothing as yet worthy of my gifts. I have led an extremely debauched life, a life of subtle sin. Raise me from this couch already redolent of death! I shall go to Mount Athos, I shall prostrate myself before the Elders that they might make of me an humble and true faithful, one of those who believe in *Wednesdays and Fridays*, and in miracles. I am ready to don the monastic habit." '

Leontiev was a man of exceptional sincerity and integrity; every word he wrote makes us feel this. This immense agony is dumbfounding by its simplicity, by its absence of any affectation and artificiality. A rationalist will see nothing surprising in this episode. 'Here is simply a man afraid of death', he will say, 'and that fear drives him to invoke supernatural powers!' It would be difficult to contradict this, for the bare facts themselves prove nothing. But anyone capable of glimpsing the spiritual truth beneath the external attributes will surely be struck by the trait of Divine Providence thus manifest in Leontiev's life. Being an act of grace, his religious crisis was like all crises of that nature. The ground had been prepared to receive the gift of grace, and there was nothing left but to consummate the transformation. The nature of this crisis determined Leontiev's religious type. His conversion was an act of grace; but he belonged nevertheless to a category of beings whom grace had not visited. The terror of corporeal death and eternal damnation was the foundation of his faith. His essentially aesthetic hatred of progress and of bourgeois civilization strengthened his passion for Byzantine Orthodoxy and the monastic life. His religious spirit was from the start essentially dualistic, and it remained so in its fundamental characteristics. His religious experience had need of oppositions and contrasts. Mortification strengthened his faith, but he had almost no feeling for charity. He accepted Christianity first of all as a religion of terror, and only later as a religion of love. In a very remark-

[62]

able letter which he addressed to a student, and which was published by the *Theological Courier*, Leontiev gave the following description of his conversion: 'What I lacked at the time was *true suffering*; there was no trace of *humility* in my heart; I had confidence in myself. I was much happier than I had been in my youth, and I was very pleased with myself. From 1869 onwards a sudden change came about; I had to put up with all kinds of misfortunes. For the first time in my life I had a clear sense of the workings of the Almighty. I aspired to obey Him. I was relying on this submission as a support against the cruel tempest unleased within me. I only lacked the *form* in which I might commune with God. The most *natural* thing for me was to submit to the *Orthodox rite*. I went to Mount Athos in order to learn to become a true Orthodox Christian, in order that the austere monks might teach me to believe. I was ready to surrender to them both my spirit and my will. However, the external assaults redoubled, and the ground was prepared in my soul. At last, the hour came when I experienced an unknown *terror*. It was not simply fear. This terror struck at once at my body and my spirit, it was the *terror of sin, the terror of death*. I am not easily intimidated. Until then I had never experienced that sort of terror, at least not with such force. *The decisive step had been taken*. I began to tremble *before God* and *before the Church*. In time the *physical* fear disappeared, but the spiritual terror remained. And more, *it only increased*.'

In fact, Leontiev never liberated himself from this religious terror; and henceforth he placed his life under the sign of Salvation. He had vowed to don the monastic habit if the Virgin restored him to health. His prayer was heard and he was healed. Henceforth he was obsessed with the desire to cut himself off from the world, to enter a monastery. This man of the Renaissance, this pagan, discovered in this way the antipodes of his nature. His life became dual: though he was still destined to live a certain time in the world, he had already responded heart and soul to the call of the monastic life.

As soon as he was on his feet again, Leontiev set out on his pilgrimage. On horseback he crossed the mountains on the way to the Elders of Mount Athos. His first visit was a brief one. He returned quickly to Salonika in search of an important document. He found it in a suitcase where he had also put away the manuscript of the novel to which he had devoted so much labour, *The River of Times*. Leontiev picked up the manuscript and suddenly threw it into the fire. Acting impulsively, he had made his first sacrifice to God, dedicating to Him that which a writer would cherish most. This scene is reminiscent of Gogol's drama, although its consequences were to prove quite different. Thus Leontiev began his new life by making a sacrifice of his literary work; but his creative instinct was not thereby extinguished for ever. On the contrary, it was to develop and receive a new lease of life.

Writing later to Alexandrov, he said: 'My best works (the *Odyssey* and *Byzantinism and Slavdom*) were written after a year and a half of communion with the monks of Athos, of ascetic study, and of a desperate struggle with my flesh.' Later, the Elders of the Optina Monastery bestowed their blessing on his work as a writer. They did not ask him to renounce it. In burning his *River of Times* Leontiev had in a way won a victory over himself. At this time he produced such a strange impression upon his friends in Salonika that a rumour spread that the Russian consul had gone mad. He gave up his consular post, informing the ambassador that he could no longer perform his duties for reasons of health, and set off again for Mount Athos where he stayed on this occasion for almost a year. Two remarkable Elders, Fathers Hieronymus and Makary became his spiritual guides. In order to keep his promise to the Holy Virgin, Leontiev begged his confessors to allow him to don the monastic habit, but the wise Elders did not heed his prayer. They were clear-sighted enough to realize that their spiritual son was not yet ready for monastic life, that his nature was still too passionate and impulsive, that he had not yet exhausted all the pleasures the world had to offer him, and that he would not be able to stand the strain of an ascetic life.

And so Leontiev went out into the world again. But in his heart of hearts he was firmly resolved to lead a monastic life sooner or later. As it was, he was no longer entirely of the world. His appearance even had changed; he no longer had the air of a man bent solely on enjoying life; he looked gaunt, and had a dejected and meditative mien. He threw off the frock-coat he abhorred so much, and donned a *kaftan*, a garment somewhat like a peasant's smock or a cassock; and he dressed in this manner until the end of his days.

Soon after, he got his discharge from the service and a pension. He settled down in Constantinople and moved about chiefly in diplomatic circles, where he was regarded as a dreamer and a man of unstable character but one who excited interest and sympathy. He was later to recall this stay in Constantinople as a happy period in his life. After his pilgrimage to Mount Athos his inner tumult had subsided. He continued to live a worldly life, which differed superficially but little from that he was wont to live. And yet a profound change had come about in him. Although he still remained an aesthete and naturalist, his outlook was wholly dominated by religious aspirations and the quest for Salvation. But while his outlook became definitively Orthodox, he did not definitely become a Christian.

From the point of view of his literary output, his stay in Constantinople was the most fruitful period of his life. There he wrote his most important work, *Byzantinism and Slavdom*. In it he fully expressed and developed his conception of the universe. He applied his philosophy of history and of society to the problems of Slav policy in the East. During this period he wrote his *Polychroniades Odyssey*, which was later published in the *Russian Courier*. But Katkov refused to publish his *Byzantinism and Slavdom* in the same review. In 1874 Leontiev took leave of Constantinople and the East. He returned first of all to Moscow, and then to Kudinovo. It was the beginning of a new, difficult and painful period of his life.

CHAPTER III

BYZANTINISM AND SLAVDOM. THE NATU-RALISTIC CHARACTER OF LEONTIEV'S SPECULATION. THE LIBERAL AND EQUA-LITARIAN PROCESS. ARISTOCRATIC MORALITY. THE AESTHETIC DOCTRINE OF LIFE

I

Leontiev's knowledge was neither extensive nor complex. His ideas were penetrating and fundamental, but they lacked richness and diversity. Unlike the Gnostic spiritual type, he quested for a life of adventure rather than for a profound and varied knowledge. Although he was a man of unusual, powerful and acute intelligence—one of the finest in Russia—Leontiev was no metaphysician. He never felt quite at home in the sphere of dialectics, and handled abstract ideas badly. That he himself realized this fact is proved by his confession, that he 'was not very expert in dialectics'. He found it hard to preserve the thread of an abstract argument; he was interested above all in 'the processes of real life'. In his work there is no evidence of a philosophical training, but every indication of his biological studies and artistic gifts. 'I confess that in writing I always tend to think in terms of human psychological experience rather than of logic; I am much more concerned with the manner in which I present the facts than with the strict continuity of the ideas them-

[67]

selves. When perusing the works of others, I tire very quickly of a purely logical exposition of abstract ideas. I can only grasp abstraction when, in the course of reading, I can suddenly visualize a concrete *image*, a living illustration, however dimly or briefly, but nevertheless a living embodiment of the alien logic forcibly thrust upon me; or again, the argument might strike an echo within me of *emotions* I had experienced. But in themselves these "principles" do not mean very much to me. . . . When people talk of the *principle of love*, I have but the vaguest notion of what they mean until I recall some living manifestations of the emotion of love. . . . Metaphysics is not my strong point.' Leontiev preferred theology to metaphysics because he could relate it to the Gospel, to the Councils, to the notion of Papal Infallibility, and other visible and apprehensible manifestations of the same order. Writing to K. N. Alexandrov, he said: 'I am not very good at metaphysics, and I am always afraid that I have interpreted something too realistically and humanly rather than philosophically. I can *feel* a more concrete psychology, but in the sphere of a more *metaphysical* psychology, I go in fear and trembling lest I fail to understand.' Indeed, in this sphere he was always ready to admit the pre-eminence and superiority of Vladimir Solovyev.

Leontiev had never been a Platonist, a contemplator of general ideas. He remained faithful to his biological training even in the religious period of his life. But his naturalistic approach to life was tempered and complicated by his aesthetic and religious criteria. In him these elements—the naturalistic, the aesthetic, and the religious—seemed to function freely and independently, without impinging upon one another, but they ultimately led him to the one great

[68]

truth in which are fused all judgments and criteria. Leontiev had an extraordinary freedom of mind, greater perhaps than that of most Russian intellects; he had no ties, his independence was complete. He was an example of that true freedom of thought which is so rare in the history of the Russian intellect. This so-called 'reactionary' was a thousand times more open-minded than most Russian 'progressivists' and 'revolutionaries'. We can only compare his intellectual freedom with that of Nietzsche. Leontiev said somewhere that 'individual freedom has only made the human personality more irresponsible and insignificant'. He established a distinction between 'the individual's *legal* freedom and the personality's *real* development—one that can occur even in a state of slavery'. He had a deep understanding of the fact that 'individualism destroys the individuality of men, provinces and nations'. Writing with the same deep penetration, he said elsewhere that 'turning a sharp corner, *we have undertaken to emancipate thought*'. And verily the whole trend of the Russian movement of 'emancipation', which was bringing freedom to the individual and society, has not only brought about the emancipation of thought but also its final enslavement. But one of Leontiev's great services was that he did really help to emancipate thought; he was an example of a 'personality', of 'an individuality's living development', as distinct from a mere individual, content with an abstract 'freedom of his person'.

In his sociological researches Leontiev aspired to be detached, objective and impervious to human sufferings. His ideal was the exact opposite of that pursued by the Russian 'subjective school of sociology'. As a sociologist he firmly eliminated morality and the gospel of love for humanity. He placed sociology in the same category as zoology, for which, incidentally, he had a taste and liking. 'There are very humane men, but no humane States. The *heart* of this or that ruler can be humane; but neither a nation nor a State is a human organism. They are organisms, it is true, but organisms of a different order; they are essentially *ideas*, incarnated in a given social structure. There is no humane heart in *ideas*. They are merciless and cruel, for they are in essence no more and no less than the clearly or dimly formulated laws of nature and history.' 'Suffering is equally the accompaniment of the process of growth and development, and of the process of disintegration. The tree of human life is afflicted with a perpetual ache. . . . *But in the social life pain is the last and most elusive of symptoms*, for it is subjective.' This passage gives us a fair idea of Leontiev's intellectual approach to the problem of the social process. And the writing of this ruthless naturalist, this objective physiologist and pathologist of human society, is given added authority by his aesthetic judgments and his religious faith. With religious pathos and aesthetic delight he affirmed the agency of iron natural necessity in human society, the objective-natural foundations of society impeding man's subjective will. *He beholds God and Beauty in these natural laws manifest throughout history.* The divine principle is revealed to him in natural necessity rather than in human freedom. In this he bears an affinity to J. de Maistre and the French counter-revolutionary Catholic school of thought, although he would appear to have had no knowledge of them. Thus Leontiev's naturalistic bias made him deny the category of freedom, the creative significance of spirit in the life of society.

Leontiev was at bottom a kindly and sensitive man, amiable and considerate in his dealings with other men. This fact is evident from his letters, from the recollections of his contemporaries, from his life itself. He showed perhaps a greater kindliness and love in his relations with people than Michailovsky, who preached a humane and heartfelt 'subjective sociology'. J. de Maistre was another example of a kindly and considerate man. His published correspondence was a source of universal surprise. People could hardly credit that one who advocated the apotheosis of the executioner, and expiation through the blood of innocent victims, should turn out to be such a fine human being. Leontiev's ruthless ideas also excited a great deal of misunderstanding about him. There is an illuminating passage about himself in a letter he wrote to A. Alexandrov: 'Although I never advocate "pure morality", and cannot bear to hear people talk of their "love for humanity", I am not, as you probably know, entirely lacking in an ethical sense and goodness.' In his *Memoirs* he speaks of that 'love for men which I never championed in writing, leaving that to others, but to whose warm and sincere impulses I was of course never a stranger. My friends are well aware of this.' And indeed, all who knew him were unanimous on this point. Leontiev liked the genuine living men whom he met in the course of his life; he disliked the notion of abstract humanity and abstract man, of abstract human good and utility. His ruthless naturalistic sociology was no obstacle to his love of living men, but it made it impossible for him to entertain any love for abstract humanity or utopias of earthly perfection. Thus Leontiev's aesthetic attitude held the notion of abstract humanity and earthly bliss in contempt, but put no barriers in the way of loving living human beings. It is important to clarify this aspect of

[71]

Leontiev's personality. This love of living beings as distinct from abstract notions of happiness was likewise an expression of his Christian belief. Society was for him an organism of a different order from the human one, and he treated it accordingly in a way other than he would have treated the human soul. In this he differed from the usual Russian approach to the problem of society,—from the sentimental approach with its exclusively subjective and moral categories. Thanks to his method, Leontiev was able to make several sociological discoveries the value of which still remains to be assessed, and which are confirmed by the living social process. 'Let us be severe in politics, cruel and ruthless even in State affairs, but let us not be exclusive in our "personal" judgments. Political severity is the expression of the might and power of the national will; an inflexibility and narrowness in personal judgments is a sign of mental weakness and poverty in the living imagination.' Hence it is clear why Leontiev was a kindly and considerate man in his private life, and a severe and ruthless sociologist in his doctrine. In Russia it is the reverse of this that is more often true. But it is also true to say that, because of his naturalistic bias and inborn paganism, Leontiev failed to grasp the whole urgency and complexity of the problem of realizing Christian truth in the life of society.

Leontiev's sociological doctrine was influenced to some extent by Danilevsky's work, *Russia and Europe*. Danilevsky was also a naturalist in his mental outlook and training, and he gave a naturalistic foundation to some of the Slavophil ideas. But he had already criticized the Slavophil passion for 'universal humanity' and 'tendency to humanitarianism'. He had already evolved a biological doctrine of culture,

[72]

treating of its stages of flowering and decline, and he instanced the European Romano-German type of historical culture as an example of a declining culture. Danilevsky developed the theory of cultural and historical types, and attempted to establish an original Slav cultural and historical type, which was to replace the Romano-Germanic type. This somewhat arbitrary and, in its pure form, inadmissible theory was yet fruitfully and originally developed by Leontiev. He found Danilevsky's outlook and method much more sympathetic than that of the older Slavophils who, indeed, had never exercised any direct influence on him. They shared in common a less intransigent attitude to the history of Europe than did the Slavophils. Thus Danilevsky provided Leontiev with a scientific method, of which he made use to elaborate a completely original structure born of an entirely different set of inner motives and interests. With a generous disinterestedness and an unselfishness peculiar to him, Leontiev acknowledged his debt to Danilevsky and attributed to him a much greater influence upon himself than was really the case, although it is undeniable that Danilevsky was an intelligent and original thinker. But Leontiev's speculation was vital and concrete. Speaking about his best work, *Byzantinism and Slavdom*, which is the sum of his whole social philosophy, he said: 'I wrote *Byzantinism and Slavdom* inspired by a sudden urge in my soul, without any scientific preparation or sufficient sources of bibliographical information. The force of the inspiration was so great at the time (in 1873), that I am now amazed at my temerity.' The impulse that started him off on that work had been provided by Eastern politics, for Leontiev was incapable of writing without some direct inspiration from life. But we must look deeper for the inner motives determining his whole philosophy of history. These motives were above all aesthetic. Leontiev had been driven to meditate deeply upon the philosophy of history, upon the destiny of societies, States and cultures, upon the mobile springs of the social process, because he had above all been shocked and wounded by a thought that had struck him as he contemplated the contemporary European scene: 'Is it not terrible, is it not a shame, to think that Moses ascended Sinai, that the Greeks built their elegant Acropoles, that the Romans waged their Punic wars, that the great and handsome Alexander, in a feathered helm, crossed the Granik and fought by Arbela, that the Apostles preached, that martyrs suffered, that poets sang, that painters painted, and that medieval knights shone in tourneys, *only to make it possible* for the French, German or Russian bourgeois, attired in his revolting and comic costume, to "sentimentalize" individually and collectively upon the ruins of that great past? . . . It would be a humiliation to humanity if that vile ideal of universal utility, mean toil and shameful prose could triumph forever!'

The image of the *bourgeoisie* impressed Leontiev as the final result of the liberal and equalitarian process which had got Europe in its grip. And he was both horrified and disgusted. Hertzen, whom Leontiev liked and who had exercised some influence upon him, had already felt the danger represented by the European bourgeoisie. But Leontiev was more acutely aware of the problem and he gave it a deeper foundation. In the West, too, men like Carlyle, Nietzsche, Ibsen, and Léon Bloy, had taken up the struggle against the conquering bourgeoisie. But Léon Bloy, like Leontiev, was the only one of them who probed the problem to its religious foundations. Leontiev experienced first of all an aesthetic, and then a religious hatred, for the idea of 'progress', which is the password into the bourgeois kingdom; he also hated the slogans of liberty and equality, which he regarded as the chief weapons in the armoury of the bourgeois State. Leontiev's attitude to Europe was, however, different from that of the Slavophils. He was almost in love with the great past of Europe. He liked those aspects of Europe which were 'beautifully expressed in its traditions: its chivalry, subtlety, and romanticism'; he loved the poetry of the Papacy as contrasted with the prose of the Western proletariat. 'There was in European life a greater variety, more lyricism, more consciousness, more reason and more passion, than in the life of former historical worlds. There were more architectural monuments, famous people, priests, monks, warriors, rulers, artists, poets; the wars were on a larger scale; the philosophy was more profound and richer; religion was incomparably more passionate (than that of the Greeks and Romans, for example); the aristocracy and the various monarchies more sharply defined than the Roman; and in general, the fundamental principles of the European State system were far more complex than those of the ancient world.' And Leontiev could not forgive Europe for having turned its back upon its noble past. This attitude had little in common with that of the Slavophils. Leontiev was not an enemy of the fundamental principles of European culture, such as Catholicism, feudalism and chivalry. He condemned the betrayal of these principles which afforded him such aesthetic delight. The bourgeoisie had defeated Catholicism, the aristocracy, and the poetry of old Europe. 'Since the Declaration of the

[75]

Rights of Man exactly a hundred years ago, there has been a steady disfigurement of man's image upon this increasingly democratic and vulgar earth.' The 'poetry of life' was at an end, and in its place there only survived a 'poetry of reflection'. The 'poetry of life' had flowered in the Middle Ages and at the time of the Renaissance. These were the epochs that Leontiev loved to the exclusion of all else. The ideal of democracy was for him 'intolerably prosaic', and he praised Hertzen for having grasped this fact. What would have happened in France had the revolutionary social ideal triumphed? 'Would the national physiognomy of the Frenchman have been renewed? Not at all. On the contrary, it would have been effaced more than ever. In place of several hundred thousand rich bourgeois, we should have had forty million petty bourgeois. By their occupation, name and social position, they would not have been bourgeois; but by their outlook, behaviour, and by all those characteristics which, apart from their political position, make up the sum of qualities requisite for the living person—by what might be termed their spiritual physiognomy or character—they would have been bourgeois.' Thus Leontiev was one of the first to discover that Socialism was spiritually of bourgeois origin. 'It is stupid to believe so blindly, as most European-educated people do to-day, in something impossible, in the final kingdom of truth and happiness upon earth, in a bourgeois and workers' paradise, in a drab and impersonal earthly paradise. . . . It is stupid and shameful for people who have some respect for *realism* to believe in such an *unreal* thing as man's happiness, even his approximate happiness. . . . It is ridiculous to uphold such an ideal which is neither compatible with historical experience, nor with the laws

[76]

and examples of natural history. Organic nature lives by variety, antagonism and struggle; and through this antagonism, rather than through an *applied uniformity*, it does achieve a measure of unity and harmony. If history is but the highest manifestation of organic life on earth, then an intelligent realist must not be either a democrat or a progressivist in the actual sense of the word. After being a realist in geology, physics and botany, it would be absurd suddenly to be transformed into a utilitarian thinker on the *threshold of sociology*. It would be foolish to worship the *orthodoxy of progress*, the idol of the progressive movement, having first of all denied every positive and restricting *mystical orthodoxy* as a sign of naïveté and backwardness.' Thus Leontiev believed that the petty and foolish dream of an earthly bliss ran counter to everything real,—to aesthetic ideals, religious beliefs, ethics and science. Man required experience to convince him that the 'progress of measured happiness' was unattainable, that it was merely a step towards further inequality and suffering. 'I have the right to despise such a pallid and unworthy humanity, without vices it is true, but without virtues also, and I have no wish to do anything to help such progress! . . . And more! If I have no power, I shall dream passionately of besmirching the ideal of equality and universal insane progress; if I have power, I shall work to destroy such a state, for I love mankind too much to wish for it such a peaceful future, perhaps, but also a mean and degrading one!' Progressive ideas are rough, simple and easily assimilated. They appeared wise and profound when they were the preserve of a few elect minds. High-minded men ennobled them with their brilliant gifts; but the ideas themselves were not only essentially erroneous but also vulgar and detestable. *Earthly*

[77]

prosperity is unmitigated nonsense, an *impossibility; the reign of proportional and universal human truth* on earth is not only an absurdity, but also a harmful *lie, an affront to the better men. The divine truth of the Gospel held out no promise of earthly happiness, preached no legal freedom,* but only an ethical, spiritual freedom attainable in conditions of the worst slavery. *There were martyrs of the faith under the Turks; but under the Belgian Constitution there is hardly room for holy men.*'

Leontiev's style reached a high degree of pathos. No one has exposed with such mastery and pungency the degradation and ugliness of the idea of an earthly equality and happiness for all men. He was indeed the great enemy of Eudaemonism. 'O hateful equality! O mean uniformity! O damned progress! O cloudy blood-soaked but picturesque mountain of world history! Since the end of the last century you are tormented by new births. And from your tortured depths a mouse only emerges. Only a complacent caricature is born of former men; *the average rational European,* attired in comic clothes that even the ideal mirror of art *cannot portray;* with his crawling utilitarian good intentions, he is petty-minded and self-deluded! No, never until our time has history beheld such a monstrous blend of mental pride when confronted with God and ethical humility before the idol of the homogeneous drab worker, *the worker only and a godless-passionless mankind!* Is it possible to love *such* a mankind? Should we not hate—not the men themselves, blind and deluded,—but such a *future* in store for them, with all the force even of our Christian soul?'

It is clear that Leontiev preferred the *organic* periods of human history, the organic structure of society, rather than the *critical* periods and the critical structure of society. He looked upon society as an organism, and its emergence from the organic stage was to him a sign of disintegration and death. The sociological and philosophical problem of history was in his eyes not only a biological but primarily an aesthetic problem. His speculations upon the sociological and philosophical problems of history were coloured by his aesthetic impressions. His consciousness established a relationship, a coincidence, of aesthetic and naturalistic experiments and criteria. This identity of aesthetic and biological judgments may be defined as the element of naturalistic optimism inherent in his outlook. But in contradiction to his prophecy, that the social revolution was inevitable, Leontiev would appear to regard the realization of Socialism and social utopias as impossible, and even contrary to man's sinful nature. Actually Leontiev's own social ideal was an even greater utopia than Socialism. The idealization of organic society is a romantic trait. The very fact of the existence of organic epochs is highly debatable.

II

What do these manifestations of European progress, which provoked Leoniev's aesthetic horror and disgust, represent from the standpoint of the social sciences and the impartial natural sciences? What do democratic levelling and confusion, the advancing reign of the bourgeoisie, represent in terms of an organic social process? Leontiev approached these problems not only as an artist and aesthete, a vehement publicist and politician, but also as a biologist and sociologist. He apparently attached a great deal of importance to his biological and sociological theory, and hoped in vain that it would become the object of a serious examination. He was not a savant or specialist; his scholarship was limited; and to the academic mind he might appear a dilettante. But then, the most profound intuitions in the sphere of social philosophy have been contributed by independent thinkers. We must therefore consider Leontiev very seriously when he speaks in the cold, impartial and austere idiom of science. 'When social science has once been forced to admit that every society and state, every nation and culture, is essentially a sort of organism, and that every organism develops through *the differentiation of the parts in the whole*, then it must also admit the reverse, that is, the fact that impending disintegration is expressed in *the confusion* of those elements which *were formerly differentiated;* and this is attributable to the great similarity of positions, rights and needs, *to the weakening of the unity* which had formerly bound together the rich variety of its component parts. The dissolution of the whole into parts, as the result of weakened unity, is the end of everything.' Like Spencer, Leontiev wished to discover the *formula* of the organic *development* of society. He was not acquainted with Spencer's work when he wrote his *Byzantinism and Slavdom*, but on reading him later he admitted that they shared a common fundamental outlook. Leontiev interpreted development in a purely naturalistic manner, without any ethical bias. But he was not content merely to try and discover the formula of the organic development of society, he was also seeking the formula of the maximum organic perfection of a given society, the formula of its high flowering. '*The idea of development* corresponds in those real and exact sciences, from which it is translated into the historical domain, to *a certain complex process,* which is, be it noted, *not infrequently the antithesis of the process of mere*

[80]

expansion and extension and, in fact, hostile to it.' The process of development in organic life may be defined as follows: '*A gradual ascent from the simple to the complex*, a gradual individualization, an *isolation from the environing world on the one hand, and from analogous and related organisms, from all analogous and related phenomena, on the other*. A gradual movement from *colourless simplicity towards original complexity*. A growing complexity in the component parts, an *enrichment of the inner content* and, at the same time, a *gradual strengthening of the unity*. Thus it appears that *the maximum point of development*, not only in organic bodies but also generally in organic phenomena, *is the maximum stage of complexity, consolidated by a certain inner despotic unity*.' The high point of organic development is reached when unity is blended with variety and a flowering complexity. But every living organism is subject not only to development, but also to disintegration and death. What is disintegration? Has it a formula? 'If we consider any development, whether that of a disease (a complex and uniform organic process) or that of a living healthy body (a complex and single organism), we shall realize that certain phenomena precede the disintegration and *death of the latter* (the organism) *and the annihilation of the first* (the process). These phenomena are: a simplification of the component parts, *a diminution in the number of distinct parts, a weakening of the central unity and strength*, and at the same time a growing *confusion*. There is a process of gradual *lowering, mixture and blending*, preceding the disruption and death, and the transformation into something of a more general character lacking any inner necessity and life of its own. Before it perishes completely there is a slackening in the individual tension of the parts as well as of the whole.

The dying organism becomes more uniform inwardly, and outwardly more like the exterior world, more analogous to its related phenomena (i.e. *more free*).' Leontiev completely identified this organic process with the social one. Disintegration, simplification and confusion are the signs of a fatal disease. The period of confused simplification coincided with that of a society's decrepitude. Equalization invariably implied senility. Thus Leontiev established three periods of organic social development: 'At first there is simplicity, then complexity, and finally a process of secondary simplification. This latter process has in turn three stages: first, inner equalization and confusion; second, further simplification achieved by eliminating certain characteristics, this being accompanied by a general disintegration; and finally, a passage towards non-organic "nirvana". This law applies to state organisms as well as to entire cultures. In them these three stages are clearly manifest: first, *a primary simplicity;* second, *a flowering complexity;* third, *a secondary and confused simplification.*'

Leontiev applied this formula to modern history. The significance of the contemporary European bourgeois, of the shocking results of liberal and equalitarian progress, was at once clear. The truth of an aesthetic experiment and judgment thus acquired a biological and sociological foundation. Europe had entered upon its third stage, that of 'secondary and confused simplification'; European societies were faced with decrepitude and death. Thus, over fifty years ago Leontiev had discovered what Spengler is now attempting to demonstrate in his own way. The period of development was at an end, and that of disintegration had begun. The so-called 'progress' expounded by contemporary liberals, democrats and socialists, is a sign of disintegration and death. The Renaissance had been Europe's age of 'complex flowering'. 'The new contact with Byzantium, with the ancient world, had at once brought Europe to the threshold of that brilliant age, which we are accustomed to call the "Renaissance", but which it would be better to call the age of the *complex flowering* of the West. An age such as this, such as the Renaissance, has been a common feature of all States and cultures; it is an age of varied and profound development, *characterized by a maximum of spiritual and political unity in the whole or the parts.*' A period of 'complex flowering' presupposed a complex, differentiated, heterogeneous and varied social structure, an inequality of conditions and classes, the existence of an aristocracy, of a strong political sense, of great men towering above the mass, of geniuses and saints. The passion for equality and confusion of values was fatal to societies and cultures. Democratic movements mark the decay of the social organism, the approach of senility and death. Leontiev had in fact discovered a law of social life analogous to the law of entropy. 'Throughout the eighteenth century Europe was gradually being *levelled* by a process of *secondary confusion*. Until the ninth century she was both *simple and confused;* now, in the nineteenth century, she again aspires to *confusion*. She has lived a millennium! She would dispense with more *morphology!* By means of this confusion she is aspiring to the ideal of *uniform simplicity*, and unable to attain it by a long way she will have to retreat and give way to others!' What is *form?* Leontiev defines it as '*the despotism of an inner idea preventing the dissolution of matter*'. He goes on to say: 'The vision perishes when it throws off the constraint of this authentic despotism. . . . Crystallization is the despot-

[83]

ism of an inner idea.' In contemporary society this despotism was no more, and with it had gone the sense of form. 'There is no logical connection between the equalitarian and liberal progressive movement and the idea of development. What is more, *the equalitarian and liberal process is the antithesis of the process of development.* In the latter case, an inner idea dominates the social material, moulding and organizing it, controlling its centrifugal and disruptive tendencies. On the other hand, the idea of progress is hostile to any kind of despotism, whether that of conditions, monasteries, wealth, and so on, and is thus nothing but a *process of disintegration*, a process of the secondary *simplification of the whole and the confusion of the component parts*. . . . The manifestations of equalitarian and liberal progress are similar to the effects of combustion, decay and the melting of ice; they may be compared to the symptoms of cholera, for example, which gradually transforms quite different people, first of all into more uniform corpses (equality), then into almost completely identical corpses (equality), and finally into the freedom of nitrogen, hydrogen, oxygen and so on.' 'In its general aspect Europe has reached the stage of *secondary confusion*, its component parts have become *much more alike and uniform*, and the complex processes of "progress" imply a complication like that of *some terrible pathological process*, gradually reducing *a complete organism* to *the secondary simplification of a corpse, skeleton and a heap of ashes!*' But 'nothing truly great, lofty and durable, is achieved through *epidemic liberty and equality, but only through a variety of situations, education, impressions and rights, in a milieu unified by some higher and sacred authority*'. For Leontiev there was a mystery attached to this naturalistic process of equalization. All contemporary forces

[84]

'appear to be only the blind instruments of that *mysterious will*, which is steadily pursuing its object of democratizing, levelling, confusing, first, the social elements of the whole of Romano-Germanic Europe, and then, perhaps, the whole of mankind'.

Leontiev established an original relationship between the progressivists and the reactionaries. Until the period of flowering complexity 'all the progressivists were right, and all the conservatives wrong'. 'Following that flowering and complex age, with the beginning of the process of simplification, of the *confusion* of outlines, that is, with the beginning of the process of growing uniformity in the various spheres, of confused conditions, of shifting and uncertain authority, of more uniform education, with the decline of the despotism of the morphological process, *it happens that, from the standpoint of the good of the state, all progressivists turn out to be theoretically wrong although they are triumphant in practice*. They are theoretically wrong because they destroy what they would mend; they are triumphant in practice because they allow themselves to drift down with the current. They triumph and achieve a popular success. On the other hand, *all conservatives and friends of reaction are theoretically right* as soon as the process of secondary simplification and confusion has begun, *for it is their desire to cure and strengthen the organism*. It is not their fault that the nation has thrown off the discipline of the abstract idea of government latent in its depths!' This was a very bold way of posing the problem, and it implied a fearless and disarming pessimism. Thus Leontiev's point of view had little in common with the ordinary run of reactionary opinion; his outlook was in any case untrammelled and far-sighted. Leontiev had in fact attempted to provide a unique biological, sociological and aesthetic foundation, for the cause of reaction. His reactionary outlook was the result of his love for the development and flowering of culture. In this consisted the originality of his world outlook, which has not so far been sufficiently appreciated. He was a Renaissance type, and for that reason he tended to be a reactionary in our own time. But he cannot be accused of obscurantism. His reactionary ethos was bound up with his love of life rather than with his disgust of it. As a reactionary he was quite unlike Pobledonostzev, for example, although the latter was more subtle and profound than is generally imagined. 'It is useless to be *merely a conservative* in our day. We may love the past but we cannot believe even in its approximate renascence.' 'We should believe in progress as a rebirth of life's burdens, as a new aspect of human suffering and difficulties, rather than as a source of unfailing improvement. *A true belief in progress* should be a *pessimistic* one, rather than a happy expectation of some new *spring*. . . . In this sense I regard myself as a much *truer* progressivist than our liberals.' Fearless thinking was, indeed, one of Leontiev's characteristics. He entertained no rosy or optimistic illusions. He looked the future straight in the face, a future that filled him with dread and disgust, and about which he prophesied much that has already proved true and is now proving true. Leontiev's aestheticism implied a pessimistic foundation, a renouncement of easy optimism. His biological bias reinforced this pessimism. He did not believe in the freedom of spirit, he was blind to it. He did not assume the absolute value of every human personality. In fact there was nothing essentially Christian about his naturalistic sociology.

[86]

Leontiev's naturalistic deductions and aesthetic criteria led him to the discovery of one and the same truth. He detected, as it were, the pre-existing harmony of natural and aesthetic laws; in other words, he realized the aesthetic significance of natural life. 'It is remarkable that the fundamental notion of aesthetics should correspond to the definition of the idea of development in material nature: unity in variety, so-called *harmony*, not only does not exclude antithesis and struggle, but on the contrary has need of them.' Thus Leontiev's system of aesthetics postulated the existence of contrasts in social life, of dark and evil forces to balance light and goodness. But this was also implied in the natural development of life; and thus Leontiev was able to affirm the universal character of the aesthetic criterion. In a remarkable letter addressed to Father Foudel he suggested the following scheme:

Mysticism (especially positive religions).	A criterion only for co-religionists; for a Christian cannot be judged by a Mussulman, and *vice versa*.
Ethics and politics.	For man only.
Biology (the physiology of human beings, animals and plants; medicine, etc.).	For the whole organic world.
Physics (chemistry, mechanics, etc.) and Aesthetics.	Of universal validity.

Therefore, in his opinion, the aesthetic criterion had a universal validity, while the ethical criterion had only a restricted one. The aesthetic criterion had an ontological pre-

eminence over the moral one in the event of a conflict between them. 'There is something enigmatic, mysterious and,
as it were, sad, about the manifestations of universal aesthetics, because it is clear to the man *who refuses to delude himself*,
how prone aesthetic laws are to clash with moral laws and
with life's apparent utilitarianism. . . . Julius Caesar was by
our standards a very immoral man. And General Skobelev
was a far greater libertine than many of our present-day
"honest toilers". But what is an aesthetically conscious man
to do in the light of these *facts*? Can he *deny* that there was a
thousand times more poetic value in Caesar and Skobelev
than in the most good-natured and honest of village
teachers?' This expressed doctrine of 'aesthetic amoralism'
suggests a comparison between Leontiev and Nietzsche. But
it would be more exact to say that, in a more profound
sense, neither of them were really amoralists. For ultimately
Leontiev valued beauty for the good he saw in it, and hated
ugliness for the evil inherent in it. In his eyes, the stage of
secondary simplification and confusion was characterized
not only by deformity but also by evil. Indeed, it would be
more just to say, that what he affirmed was not a form of
social and historical amoralism but rather a different kind of
morality incommensurable with individual morality, and
founded upon the denial of the value of the personality. One
fact surprised and fascinated him, that 'beauty' could be the
property equally of 'a crystal and Alexander the Great, a tree
and an ascetic sitting beneath it'. 'The aesthetic criterion is
applicable to *everything*, beginning with minerals and ending
with man. Hence it is also applicable to distinct human
societies as well as to sociological and historical problems.
Where there is much poetry, there will inevitably be much

faith, much religiosity and even much *living* morality. . . . The aestheticism of life is far more important than the reflected aestheticism of art. . . . Given a life of splendour, richness and variety, of antagonism between the divine (religious) and the passionate-aesthetic (demoniac) forces, manifestations of genius will be *reflected* in art.' Thus Leontiev identified beauty with life and being, and attached a primary value to aesthetic values. They comprehended ultimately all other values, whether social, political, moral or religious. The clash of divine and demoniac principles had its aesthetic justification, but it also served the higher goal and plenitude of life. The very antagonism between aesthetics and morality helped to make life more complete.

Thus Leontiev propounded an original sort of aesthetic Pantheism, which was bound to clash with his religious theism. He had evolved a peculiar form of natural philosophy, but he failed to develop it further and to give it a gnosiological foundation. Its characteristic features were, however, an identification of aesthetics with biology, of beauty with life. 'A culture is great and powerful only when its historical landscape abounds in *beauty and poetry. Unity in variety* is the general and fundamental law of beauty.' Leontiev might be called an amoralist only in a specific sense; but in reality, he affirmed the identity of aesthetics and morality, and propounded, like Nietzsche, a special sort of morality. In his eyes, the very existence of morality postulated the aesthetic perquisites of variety and contrast. 'Given variety, there will be *morality*. . . . For would not the triumph of the universal happiness, were it realizable even for a short while, lead to the destruction of all morality. Charity, goodness, justice, self-sacrifice, these could not exist without sorrow, inequality, wrong, cruelty, and so forth.' The necessity and rightness of inequality, contrast and variety, was the fundamental idea of Leontiev's life; it was an idea that combined all the aspects of aesthetics, biology, sociology, morality and religion. He had glimpsed that ontological truth, which affirms that being is inequality, and inequality is being. He did not preach amoralism, but only what was in his judgment the higher morality of inequality, of a life consecrated to beauty. He was religiously convinced that God Himself desired inequality, contrast and variety. It followed that the aspiration for equality, confusion and uniformity, was both atheistic and hostile to life. Thus a demoniac love of beauty was for him a more godly thing than a levelling morality. Hence he attributed a positive and objective social, political, moral and religious significance to all his aesthetic judgments. These latter had all the weight of a complete spiritual affirmation; but it is also true to say, that his outlook was more in keeping with that of an ancient Greek than with that of a Christian.

'In my eyes, a strong man has a *validity of his own,* a vivid historical and psychological phenomenon has a *value of its own.* I value Bismarck as a *phenomenon,* as a *character,* as an *example* to many, even though he may be our implacable enemy.' This was first of all, an aesthetic judgment, then a moral one, and finally a religious and ontological one. '*Only when the State is strong, and communal forces potent, is there any abundance of vital poetry, of poetry in general.* The power of the State is a hidden iron scaffolding upon which the great artist —we may call him history—fashions mighty and elegant forms of human culture.' Here again his aesthetic judgment coincided with criteria of another order, social, political and moral. 'In whatever form beauty actually manifests itself, it cannot help but strengthen national life by adorning and glorifying it.' This was another example of his integrated judgment. But here are some passages which would appear to justify the popular conception of Leontiev as a political amoralist and inveterate disciple of Machiavelli. 'Good men are not infrequently worse than bad ones. Personal honesty and an entirely free morality may be *individually* attractive and worthy of respect, but there is *nothing political, no organizing quality*, in these precarious things. Sometimes very good men cause the State great injury, if their political education has been falsely conducted. But sometimes characters, like Gogol's Chichikov, may prove to be incomparably more valuable to the nation as a whole.' 'I have nothing to say about *sympathy, suffering*, etc. All these heartrending phrases lead nowhere. A frank reliance on *egotistical interests is much more to the point*.' 'What has an honest and real historical science to do with discomforts, needs, despotism, sufferings? These unscientific sentimentalities, so prevalent in our day, so incapable and prosaic into the bargain, are all a waste of time! Why should I concern myself in this domain with the very groans of men? . . . The State is like a tree, which reaches its full stature, bloom and fruitfulness, in obedience to a certain mysterious and independent despotic willing of its inherent idea.'

These ideas, at the foundation of Leontiev's sociological investigations, were diametrically opposed to subjectivist and ethical sociology. But did that necessarily mean that Leontiev himself was an amoralist? To his way of thinking, there was a higher morality and truth in a cold, severe and ruthless attitude to human nature, than in the subjective human will, in utilitarian sentiments and in the idea of human happiness. His was, in fact, a different and hardly Christian morality. Nor did he show himself an amoralist when he exclaimed, 'Leaders are not bred by the Parliamentary system, but by *real freedom,* that is, *by a certain measure of autocratic freedom.* One must *know* how to rule without modesty!' These were the views of one who championed the morality of power, of chiefs and leaders, against that of the masses and of autonomous personalities. 'Where this lawful and sacred right of coercion over our will has grown weak both in the consciousness of those who coerce and in the hearts of those who are coerced, wherever both the ability to govern boldly and the capacity of submitting with love and fear have been lost, there will be no strength, no duration, no stable and lasting order.' This passage again demonstrated the fusion of aesthetic, moral, political and biological criteria. '*A certain degree of cunning is essential in politics.*' 'Mysticism is, so to speak, more expedient and "rational" than petty utilitarian atheism.' 'Their ideal—*the European bourgeois*—resembles them. It is not that of the peasant or gentleman, the warrior or priest, the Briton or Basque, the Cherkess or Tyrolean, the marquis clothed in velvet and feathers, or the trappist in hair-cloth or the prelate in brocade, but merely that of the *average man.* These people are above all ignorant of the laws of beauty, for the average type is invariably less aesthetic, less expressive, less intensively and extensively fine, less heroic, than more complex and more completely developed types. *This is unscientific because un-artistic.* The aesthetic criterion is the *only* sure one, because it is the only *general* one applicable to all societies, religions and epochs.'

Leontiev was convinced that the average bourgeois type

was not only anti-aesthetic but also nihilist in its implications, that is, ultimately amoral, anti-ontological, atheistic.
And here is another vivid passage which confirms my interpretation of Leontiev: 'It is precisely in the *visible* social *injustice* that the invisible social *truth* has its roots,—a profound
and mysterious organic truth of social health which cannot
be contradicted with impunity even by the best and most
charitable sentiments. Morality, like politics, has its own
sphere and limitations. The effect of introducing politics, in
an excessive way or for the sake of personal gain, into private
affairs, is to kill the *real* inward morality. And when morality
is applied too naïvely and enthusiastically in political and
social matters its effect is sometimes to shake and destroy the
political structure of the State.' '*Politics is not ethics*. . . . And
what are we to do about it? It has its own laws, which are
independent of the *ethical* ones.' '*Great social injustices are
necessary for the development of great and strong characters.*'
Leontiev's politics had their own moral laws, and these were
quite unlike the laws of personal morality, which not infrequently undermined the State and society, and lowered the
standards of life. His morality justified slavery, coercion and
despotism, in return for political and national power, flowering culture, originality of spirit. He praised the 'chronic despotism', *the unequal and heterogeneous despotism*, which was
accepted and tolerated more or less by all, willing or unwilling, out of love or fear, because of profit or self-denial. He
believed that despotism was the foundation of a mighty and
flowering life, of truth and beauty. In a state of simplified
confusion, of homogeneity, there could be no original
thinkers or geniuses. There was an aesthetic as well as an
ethical necessity for heterogeneity. 'For one who does not

believe that bliss and absolute truth are man's vocation on earth, there is nothing terrible in the idea that millions of Russians have been obliged to live under the pressure of "three atmospheres",—that of the bureaucracy, that of the landowners and that of the Church,—if only to enable Pushkin to write his *Eugene Onyegin* and *Boris Gudounov*, the Kremlin to be built, and Suvorov and Kutouzov to win their national victories. . . . For glory, military glory. . . . Yes, the military glory of the Empire and the people, their art and poetry, are undeniable *facts*, the *real phenomena* of real nature. And as objectives they are both lofty and attainable. But as to the godlessly righteous and vapidly blissful humanity, to which you aspire in your tortuous "modern" way, such a humanity would be actually vile.'

These extraordinarily forceful words implied a definite ethical consciousness; and they propounded a specific morality, which was not shared by the majority of Russian intellectuals, Tolstoy and the Russian populists. It was a morality of values rather than one of human happiness,—one which exalted supra-personal values above personal happiness. The attainment of higher, supra-personal and superhuman ends justified the sacrifices and sufferings of history. It would be an obvious error to define this simply as amoralism. Nor was Nietzsche an amoralist when he opposed the ethics of 'far away love' to that of 'love your neighbour'. It was simply a different system of ethics. But we might ask, did it correspond with Christian ethics? Leontiev was never fully able to accept the Gospel ethics. Thus he remained a pagan in his attitude to history and society, exalting values for their own sake over and above man.

Leontiev was the champion of the morality of strong,

powerful, and heroic individualities, as opposed to that of the average utilitarian and democratic man. 'On the one hand, I respect the qualities of the aristocracy; on the other, the rude simplicity of the peasantry. Count Vronsky and Onyegin, the soldier Karatayev and, let us say, Turgeniev's Biryouk, are all in their way better than the "average" bourgeois type, to which progress is now gradually reducing both the high and the low, the marquis and the shepherd.' He had not only an aesthetic but also an ethical horror of the prosaic religion of universal utility. In his eyes, the idea of universal happiness was immoral. It is essential to stress this fact in order to understand Leontiev more deeply. 'These are but the *instruments of confusion*—a gigantic grinding-mill, pounding *all and sundry in one mortar of pseudo-humane vulgarity and prose; it is all a complex algebraic method aiming to reduce all and sundry to a common denominator*. The methods of equalitarian progress are complex; *its aim is vulgar,* and its thought, ideal and influence, are all elementary. Its goal is *the average man*, a tranquil bourgeois among millions of other tranquil mediocrities.'

These words were charged with aesthetic and ethical indignation. Leontiev was a resolute opponent of the ethics of the autonomous personality. 'European thought worships man *because he is man*, not because he is a hero or prophet, Tsar or genius. Instead of worshipping a *specific and completely developed personality*, it worships simply the individuality of *each* man, and it aspires to make *each personality* happy (here on earth), just, tranquil, arrogantly honest and free within the limits of a *certain* morality. This search for an all-human justice and truth, originating not in a *positive* profession of faith but in what the philosophers call an *autono-*

mous morality, is the poison, the most subtle and potent of all plagues, slowly at work decomposing all European societies.' Leontiev based his ethical system not upon the value of each personality, but upon that of a personality's high quality or assortment of qualities. His was an ethics of quality rather than of quantity. His moral consciousness was anti-Kantian. Aristocratic morality is a special sort of morality rather than a form of amoralism. As a *conscious* exponent of aristocratic and qualitative ethics, Leontiev said: 'Not all virtues are equally useful to all classes of men: a strong sense of personal dignity gives rise to chivalry in the higher ranks of society, but when diffused among the masses it excites insurrections like those of the Paris "blousards". . . . *In this case also a uniform development turns out to be anti-social.'* He failed to understand, both from the aesthetic and ethical standpoints, why 'it is easier to obey a shoemaker than a *priest* or a *warrior* blessed by a priest'. He detested equally 'the savage communard who sets fire to the treasures of the Tuileries and the unbelieving guardian of capital'. 'If human societies would survive, they must live in a state of *fear and love*. . . . A blend of fear and love in the heart . . . a sacred fear in the face of certain ideal *frontiers*, a loving fear when confronted with certain *persons*, a feeling of reverence at the sight of certain *material objects,* such as an icon, a Cathedral, Church furniture.' The completely autonomous type of man, who feels no 'sacred fear' in the face of higher things, was morally a low spiritual type. 'Nothing can be done without *coercion*. It is untrue that one can live without it. *Coercion not only conquers but also convinces many people, when it has an idea behind it.* In moments of difficulty and danger in historical life society invariably prostrates itself before

[96]

strong men who know how to command and coerce the intractable,
rather than before the orators and journalists, the pedants
and the law-abiding!' This was definitely an ethical doctrine
of force quite unlike the prevalent Russian moral consciousness, which denied and treated with suspicion the moral
foundations of force. In any case this system of ethics had
little in common with the Gospel.

Thus Leontiev was an enemy, a formidable and implacable enemy, of humanist ethics. He devoted the whole
energy of his passionate temperament, his keen mind, his
unusual gifts, to denying all connection between Christianity
and humanism. He foretold the end and ultimate results of
humanism. He maintained that humanistic freedom would
exhaust man and transform him into non-being. He did not
love man's individualities for their own sake, but he did
respect original and powerful individualities,—'the exclusive,
distinct, powerful and expressive development of characters.'
Individualism and autonomism, on the other hand, were
hostile to such a development of characters or individualities. A personality's 'real freedom' was conceivable even
under torture. Leontiev's predilection for strongly expressed
and original characters was illustrated by his judgments in
the case of the dissenter Kurtin and the cossack Kuvaytzev.
Kurtin had killed his own son as a sacrifice to God. He made
him put on a white shirt and then wounded him several
times in the abdomen. Actually he loved his son, but committed the crime in a state of religious ecstasy. The cossack
Kuvaytzev, on the other hand, used to keep the severed hand
and finger, the hair and also the dress of his deceased love,
under his mattress. Both Kurtin and Kuvaytzev were
brought to trial. 'Of course, no one will dispute the right of

[97]

the court', Leontiev said, 'to punish such acts. But an ordinary court, like the just repressive action of the police, is but a manifestation of an "external truth". But neither a government court, nor the *court* of so-called *public opinion*, nor police repression, can exhaust the infinite rights of the personal spirit, whose depths are not always easily accessible to the general rules of the law and to the general epidemic opinions of people. A judge is obliged to punish acts which disturb the social order; but life is only powerful and fruitful where there is good, deep and original soil even for its illegal products. Kurtin and Kuvaytzev might with greater reason be the heroes of a poem than the most honest and respectable judge who very legally condemned them.' Leontiev's gaze, 'so full of hatred for certain soulless and sterile aspects of contemporary European progress,' turned to Kurtin and Kuvaytzev as examples of 'characteristic tragedy in the life of the people'. This was a clear indication of the nature of Leontiev's aesthetic and moral tastes.

His sociological and ethical doctrine was diametrically opposed to that of Mikhailovsky. He maintained that the powerful development of the personality postulated a differentiated and complex social structure. The process of 'simplified confusion' brought the personality's flowering to an end and left it exhausted. The levelling process in society killed both social and personal originality. Mikhailovsky's individualism, on the other hand, insisted upon the equality and fusion of social classes, and was accordingly unpropitious to the personality. Leontiev's point of view has been confirmed by investigators of different type, such as Simmel, for example, in his work, *Social Differentiation*. But besides discovering a sociological truth, Leontiev also evolved an

[98]

ethical one. He affirmed that supra-personal values, such as religion, culture, the State, were higher than personal happiness; that personal values should be subordinate to supra-personal ones. But Leontiev's consciousness was limited by his failure to grasp the significance of the freedom of the spirit, and by the fact that his outlook was naturalistic rather than spiritual. He was not aware of the full implications of the religious problem of man. He was inclined to forget that Christianity affirmed the absolute value of every human personality.

IV

Leontiev was prophetically aware of the impending social world revolution. In this he was totally unlike the Slavophils, who had no premonition of any catastrophe. He was acutely conscious of the fact that the old order of the world, for all its wealth of beauty, greatness, holiness and genius, was collapsing. He regarded its collapse as inevitable. In his eyes there was no way of arresting this process of simplifying confusion in Europe. But he still had hopes of Russia and the East. Before his death he had lost even this hope. 'Death must come some time; no earthly social organism, no State, culture or religion, can escape ultimate destruction and death.' Leontiev was fond of 'destiny', and he extracted more aesthetic enjoyment from the agency of 'fatal forces' than from conscious human actions. Like Nietzsche, he had the *amor fati*. 'The fulfilment of historic destinies is more dependent upon *something* higher and inapprehensible than on conscious human agency.' He had no sympathy with the aesthetics of human freedom. He denied the agency of the free human spirit in history. In this respect he had some affinity with the school of De Maistre and Bonald. He had the sentiment that the 'fatal forces' were working against him. There was a decline in the world of 'everything ecclesiastic, everything autocratic, everything aristocratic, every bastion of former originality and rich spiritual variety.' '*All is being reduced to a common denominator,* to some sort of average European type of society and to the domination of some sort of average man. And all things will obey this tendency until they blend into one All-European Republican Federation.'

The revolution was, in fact, a process of 'universal assimilation', and it was widespread. Only a person, 'who has not learnt how to read the living book of history,' could have any faith in the future of the Monarchical principle in twentieth-century Europe. Leontiev foresaw that Liberalism was inevitably preparing the way to Socialism, and he foretold with remarkable insight the character of the impending state. 'That far too *mobile* order, which gave mankind the nineteenth-century ideas of progress, equality and emancipation, is most unstable, and, despite all the temporary and beneficial efforts of conservative reaction, must end either in a universal catastrophe or *in a slow and profound transformation of human societies on the basis of completely new principles,— principles not only no longer liberal, but, on the contrary, extremely repressive and tyrannical. Perhaps slavery will return once more, assuming a different form, very likely that of a rigid subservience of persons to small and large communities, and of these in their turn to the State.*' Speaking of social forms in the future, Leontiev affirmed that '*they will not be liberal. . . .* In any case, this new culture will be very oppressive for many, and the men of the twentieth century, which is already so near to us, far from kneading it from the sugar and rose-water of measured freedom and humanity, will compound it of something else, of something terrifying even and unfamiliar'. Leontiev had early grasped the fact, and he had grasped it better than others, that Socialism would have the effect of transforming humanism into anti-humanism. Therefore he preferred Socialism to Liberalism and democracy. With Socialism the disease was approaching its conclusion, and it might very well turn into its opposite; it might prove to be the beginning of a rebirth. Leontiev was particularly unjust in his treatment of Liberalism. In his opinion, Socialism was 'performing an unconscious service for the reactionary organization of the future'. 'Do you think, gentlemen liberals, that a monument will be erected in *your* memory? No! The Socialists have everywhere a great contempt for your moderate liberalism. . . . And however much they may attack the *real conservatives* or the conservative forms and methods most unfavourable to them, *yet they will have need of all the essential aspects of the conservative doctrine.* They will have need of *fear*, they will have need of *discipline*, they will have need of *the tradition of obedience,* of *the habit of submission*. Having re-created their economic life, *but not satisfied with anything here on earth,* the peoples will flame anew with the fires of *mystical teachings.*'

These words are truly prophetic. Thus it has come to pass with Russia. Leontiev had grasped the emptiness and insignificance of sentimental humanism. 'Socialism is now apparently inevitable, at least, *for a section of mankind*. But quite apart from the suffering and injury which its triumph might cause to the vanquished, the victors themselves will soon understand, however well and solidly they might establish themselves, that they are still far from achieving prosperity and peace. *And that is like twice two makes four,* and for this reason: these victors of the future will prove to be *either freer* and more liberal than we are, *or, on the contrary,* their laws and institutions will be incomparably more repressive than ours, more severe, more tyrannical, more *terrifying* even. The life of these *new men* must ultimately prove to be far more oppressive and unhealthy than the life of good conscientious monks in austere monasteries.' Thus Leontiev had penetrated deeply into the dialectic of the social process. He was a great enemy of all illusions. 'No, there is no way of eliminating violence from the historical life. To attempt to do so would be like claiming to remove one of the prismatic colours from the rainbow of cosmic life. That colour, that great category of life, would only return in a new and more forcible form. The *plague* will almost disappear only to give way to cholera.'

It was an error on Leontiev's part to identify freedom and equality. But he did so, and despised them equally. He looked upon freedom as an exclusively negative concept. He predicted the advent of a great leader and mighty dictator in a 'Socialist' France. He wished that, in France, 'the Jacobin (liberal) Republicanism would prove to be unstable when confronted, not with the *monarchical reaction,* but with the *communard anarchy. . . .* The triumph of *a more serious commune than the temporary one of* 1871, would indubitably demonstrate both *the impotence of the "right", sincerely applied in life (the more sincerely, the worse!), and the impossibility for the people to organize itself anew on the principles of economic equality alone.* Thus the political organisms, which are still destined to *survive,* will be obliged to adopt new ways of

life quite unlike those followed by Europe since 1789.'
Leontiev foresaw not only a world revolution but also a
world war. He predicted the advent of Fascism. He lived in
the presentiment of the catastrophic rhythm of history. He
had, on the whole, a strongly developed sense of history. He
'preferred the complexity and drama of *history* to the sense-
lessness of an earthly absolute'.

Leontiev did not seek the Kingdom of God upon earth,
the reign of ultimate truth. He preferred the drama of history with all its contradictions, contrasts, good and evil,
light and shadow, striving and struggle. In this respect he
was not a typical Russian. He was a stranger to the Russian
quest for universal salvation, the salvation of all men and of
the world. He was a westerner, too, in his historical sense, in
his cultural and social judgment. He loved 'cultural values',
though he never employed that particular expression. The
salvation he sought was a personal one rather than a social or
universal one. He fused the aesthetic, the naturalistic, and the
religious elements, in his approach to the social process.
*What he interpreted from the aesthetic standpoint as the deformed
image of the bourgeoisie, and from the biological standpoint as the
process of decay and death, revealed itself to him from the religious
standpoint as the end foretold in the Evangel and the Apocalypse.*
And he was gratified aesthetically to discover that the Christian Apocalyptic prophecies did not speak so much of the
ultimate truth on earth as of the withering of love and the
victory of the anti-Christian principles. His aesthetic ethos
required the existence of a dualism of good and evil, tragedy
and suffering. The thesis of a naturalistic sociology and philosophy of history, affirming the decay and death of all
nations, states and cultures, has not yet acquired a sufficiently

universal character to be treated Apocalyptically. But history has brought about the unification of mankind, the unification of nations and cultures. We are on the threshold of universal history, when decay and death will embrace the whole world, the whole world culture. When Leontiev had finally lost his faith in Russia, he exclaimed: '*To put an end to history, having destroyed humanity;* by the spread of universal equality and universal freedom to make man's life quite intolerable on this globe. *For then there will be no new savage tribes, no old dormant cultures any more on the earth.*' He could not reconcile poetry with the exact sciences and the machine. He did not seek salvation, complexity and variety, in creativeness, but in conservatism and reaction. This was the foundation of his Byzantine doctrine and of his views on Russia's mission, but we shall discuss these aspects later. In his poetic vision of states, of their power and violence in the past, Leontiev was guilty of romantic exaggeration. He idealized historic aristocracy, confusing it with spiritual aristocracy.

V

How shall we estimate the scientific and philosophical value of Leontiev's doctrine? The critical thought of to-day will fasten first of all on the errors of method inherent in his system. The Neo-Kantians, and especially the followers of Rickert and Dilthey, would protest against his naturalistic interpretation of the social sciences. I am myself not a partisan of Rickert's gnosiological scholasticism. And I am inclined to regard the extreme methodological trends in modern philosophical criticism as a sign of decay in philosophical thought, as a sort of denial, perhaps, of the great ontological problems. But we cannot ignore the inner contradiction implicit in the naturalistic trend of Leontiev's thought. In fact, his social doctrine is only superficially objective and impartial. Actually, it is extremely passionate and arbitrary. It is a blend of nineteenth-century enthusiasm for the natural sciences and positivism, and of an inspired modern spirit which has forged ahead of its environment. Leontiev's philosophical culture was not equal to his daring intuitions and forecasts. Thus the remarkable theory from which he evolved some irrefutable truths had unfortunately rather shaky foundations. We may define his theory as one of *social morphology*, for it established beyond doubt a relationship between the forms of social life. Many of his propositions have an objective value. But Leontiev failed to discover social ontology. He failed to pass outside the sphere of social phenomenology. His philosophy is not adapted to probe the ontological foundations of society. He examines this latter as he would an organism, noting the recurrence and the relations of its forms. The most remarkable of his propositions is that in which he establishes a connection between the flowering complexity of society and its differentiation or morphological diversity, on the one hand; and between social decay and simplifying confusion, on the other. But what is the cosmic and ontological significance of this thesis? In the life of nature as well as in that of human societies there is a struggle going on between the chaotic and the cosmic forces. The supremacy of the cosmic principles within a society determines its complex and differentiated hierarchical structure. On the other hand, the supremacy of the chaotic principles leads to social simplification and confusion, to the collapse of the hierarchical system. There is some justification in regarding the stormy social manifestations of the ideal of equality as a sort of resurgence of the chaotic elements bent on overthrowing the cosmic hierarchical organization of society. Thus the decay and death of social organisms is accompanied by the breakdown of their cosmic structure and by a partial return to chaos. In this light, the processes of democracy would appear to signify the preponderance of the chaotic over the cosmic elements, helping towards a fusion, towards the suppression of the barriers and distances which were the scaffolding of the whole. For this reason, the process cannot be considered either as a development or a progress. It may lead to a primitive state of life or it may transform society into a formless mass. It may, again, prove fatal to the human personality. It is the death of all good culture. That is one of the aspects of this process. Leontiev's intuition and perspicacity in perceiving this were truly amazing. He did so, first of all, from the aesthetic standpoint, and then from the naturalistic sociological one.

But there is another aspect of democratic progress, that of the absorption into the cosmos of chaotic forces which are only outwardly repressed. This makes it possible for quantities to be raised to a higher qualitative level. Leontiev failed, however, to grasp this metaphysical problem clearly. He pressed the analogy between a society and a biological organism too far. Hence he tended to look upon the fatal process of simplifying confusion as foregone and inevitable. He disregarded the agency of man's living spirit in history. He went so far as to invest Providence with a naturalistic character, to identify it with physical laws. He failed to perceive that social life was not only natural but also spiritual. In sum, Leontiev did not understand the mystery of freedom;

it had no appeal for him. His bankruptcy lay precisely in this, and he shared this bankruptcy with every biological conception of the universe. It explains why he did not value the freedom of the human spirit revealed in Christianity. For the same reason, he identified freedom with the rising principle of equality. This was the chief source of his metaphysical and moral error; it led him to deny the rights of man, although their origin must be sought in the spiritual and immortal nature of the human being. He failed to establish any connection between spiritual freedom and Christianity, between spiritual freedom and the Christian Revelation, with its exaltation of man. It never entered his head that he might interpret the death and disintegration of the ancient world in *another* way; that he might regard them as a means whereby Christianity discarded the oppression of the pagan order. In truth, Leontiev's attitude to history and society was itself pagan. But his stormy revolt against humanism had a truth and value of its own, although he had no conception of a truly religious attitude towards man. There was great originality in the aesthetic doctrine of life, which he elaborated and which he applied to society. In his day, aestheticism was a new phenomenon, and it helped to create a gulf between him and his contemporaries. But he did not live to share in the more subtle aesthetic developments of the *fin de siècle* and the early years of the twentieth century. If he had lived to feel and experience this 'decadence', then he would most certainly have made his almost too simple theory of 'simplifying confusion' and of 'the senile corruption' of societies more complex and involved. He would have seen that, in periods of 'decadence', in the autumn of great cultures, these cultures achieve their highest degree of complexity, and display a wealth unknown to the 'periods of flowering'. But Leontiev failed to realize this. Leontiev's doctrine, of which *Byzantinism and Slavdom* was the most complete expression, embraced the quest for a full and beautiful life as well as the quest for salvation. The union of these two fundamental trends of thought incited Leontiev to reflections which were at once audacious, ruthless and profound. We have to thank him for posing the problem of the decadence of societies, cultures and States. There were points of resemblance between his theories and those of Gobineau, but Leontiev did not share in any sense the latter's racial theories.

CHAPTER IV

THE MONASTIC URGE. AESTHETICISM *VERSUS* ASCETICISM. POVERTY AND SICKNESS. LIFE IN MOSCOW. THE OPTINA MONASTERY. THE SECRET VOWS. DEATH. SPIRITUAL SOLITUDE AND ISOLATION. RELATIONS WITH VLADIMIR SOLOVYEV. VIEWS ON RUSSIAN LITERATURE.

I

The intermediate period between Leontiev's return from the East and his entry into the Optina Monastery was the hardest and most painful experience of his life. He was afflicted with every kind of difficulty, material, moral and physical. Inwardly, his life was entirely dominated by his desire to take monastic vows. A bitter struggle ensued between his religious resolve and his essentially pagan nature, his 'aesthetic demon'. In the atuumn of 1874 he went down to the Optina Monastery, which was situated some fifty miles from Kudinovo. There he met the Elder Ambrose, who was destined to exercise a decisive influence upon his spiritual life. He also met Father Clement Zederholm, whose friend he was to become, and to whom he later devoted a whole book. Leontiev's mother has related that, when she took her son to visit the Optina Monastery as a young boy, he was beside himself with joy. She even said that she had heard him exclaim: 'Never bring me here again or I might stay forever!' Thus the boy would seem to have had a presentiment of his future destiny.

In November of 1874, Leontiev also paid a visit to the Nicolo-Ugrevsky Monastery near Moscow. He began by putting up at a hotel, but before long he had moved to a cell and had donned the habit of a novice. He attempted to graduate in the austere school of monastic obedience, to execute the heaviest material labours. But this novitiate did not last long, some six months in all. He failed to find the peace he desired in the monastery; he was still unfitted for monastic life; he still had a longing for life in the East, for Constantinople. He wrote to Gubastov from the monastery as follows: 'I see with despair that it is not apparently God's will that I should return there (to Constantinople). Only there I have a sense of being alive: elsewhere I am humbly acquiescent, and learn perforce to thank God for pain and boredom.' In another letter to Gubastov he wrote: 'My thoughts keep turning to you in the Bosphorus, to Hertzegovina or Belgrad, to Moscow or Petersburg; and sometimes this silence and this world are hard to bear. Hence I came here to pray for a little while, in order to *deaden* this longing for life and glamorous struggle.' Yes, to deaden it. But to the very end he was unable to overcome his dual-nature. The 'longing for life and glamorous struggle' persisted in him. And the clash of his monastic vows with this longing was a source of torment to him. He did not enter spiritually into the monastic life, but experienced it aesthetically as a contrast with the life of the world.

There was no peace for him anywhere, no corner into which he could retire. As a writer he lacked success and influence. His remarkable work, *Byzantinism and Slavdom*, passed unnoticed. Materially his life was equally unsatisfactory: he was involved in debts and felt the pinch of need to which his letters bear witness. He could not find a situation for himself. His estate brought him no income, and its affairs were so muddled that it was in danger of being publicly auctioned. But he could not give up his gentleman's life. He always kept a number of servants. After dinner he had to have a good cigar. He had his love affairs. Neither his religious conversion nor Mount Athos banished his passion for women. He fell in love, and women fell in love with him. But his conscience tormented him, and so did the fear of punishment hereafter. He had periods of spiritual depression. His letters to Gubastov at that time were painful reading. 'It would seem that everything *living is at an end* as far as I am concerned. . . . Everything around me is dissolving. . . . There is nothing more to expect, for everything has been wept for. long ago; there is nothing to enrapture, and what is there to lose???' 'I grow smaller, tamer, dimmer for the world. I cannot adequately describe my apathy.' Now and again he gave vent to a cry of despair about his unbearably difficult position:'Help me, friends, help me, for things are in a very bad way.' But elsewhere he wrote to Gubastov: 'I thank God sincerely for many things, almost for all, especially for the great fortitude He nourishes within me in such appalling circumstances.' Leontiev was haunted, too, by the spectre of death. He believed that the year 1877 would prove fatal to him. He was so absorbed in his personal experiences that the Balkan war left him indifferent. Writing to Gubastov he remarked that he 'rarely had a mean', that he 'was invariably crowned either with thorns or roses'.

[111]

In 1879, after persistent efforts to assure his existence, he was sent to Warsaw as an assistant editor of Prince Golytzin's *Warsaw Diary*. In the articles he wrote for this paper he displayed a talent for political journalism. His temper was becoming increasingly reactionary. The revolutionary tendency apparent in Russian society incited his violent reprobation. The columns of *The Warsaw Diary* began to resound with the somewhat unpleasant notes of a typically reactionary and conservative crusade. As a thinker Leontiev became less open-minded and original. In the strict sense of the term, he belonged to no camp, to no particular movement. 'I belong to no party, to no creed; I have a doctrine of *my own*.' The conservatives and the Slavophils treated him as an artist, as a romantic figure, in fact not seriously. He even ascribed his lack of success to the fact that he was not involved in any particular movement. But he became more and more the vehicle of that conservative and reactionary style which finally dominated the age of Alexander III. It was an ugly and vulgar style enhanced only by Leontiev's unusual talent. His deeply rooted revulsion to anything 'left' made him identify himself too closely with the 'right' which was not a very enviable position in Russia. Leontiev was aware of a 'dark' corner in his soul which had 'never penetrated into the illuminated circle of *The Moscow News* and *The Russian Messenger*'. That was, indeed, the most interesting and original aspect of his soul. What business had *The Moscow News* with Leontiev's ideas, with his crazy romanticism, with his aestheticism, with his unpractical radicalism which had no application to life. The 'right' politicians had no use for him. Katkov grudgingly put up with him. Leontiev was himself aware that he worked *on sufferance*. He was hardly accessible to and of little use for, practical ends, even, though they were reactionary ones. He was interpreted in a vulgar fashion. And it is sad to think that sometimes he sank to that vulgar level of reaction which ill expressed the character of his profound, radical, noble and aristocratic doctrine. In the right camp there were no truly spiritual aristocratic elements, Leontiev was merely a journalist and wrote in the newspapers exclusively to earn his living. But in his articles he attempted to expound his most sacred and profound thoughts. He was incapable of developing his ideas systematically, and it is the pungent formula, and the odd neatly coined phrases, scattered here and there in his short articles, that really stand out.

But every now and again this original and independent thinker relapsed into common reactionary journalism, taking refuge in trite formulas. This was most apparent in his articles in *The Warsaw Diary*. In Warsaw Leontiev was agreeably impressed by the bearing of the Russian army. He had an old liking for army men, whom he preferred to civilians. His ideal had always been military rather than civilian. He was fair in his relations with Poles, he even liked them. But he worked on *The Moscow Diary* only a few months. He returned to Kudinovo on leave, in a state of collapse. Then *The Warsaw Diary* got into financial difficulties, and Leontiev had to leave it altogether. His material failures and his sicknesses threw him into a despondent state of mind. But finally, a friend of his, Philipov got him a position in the Moscow Censorship Committee. He was six years a censor, and it proved a most trying time for him. From the literary point of view, it also turned out to be his least productive period.

In the letters he wrote to Philipov, there is a note of distress, fatigue, bitterness and sorrow. He would like to have had 'some seventy-five silver roubles a month *till he died, and nothing to do.* That would be the height of bliss! . . . What happiness! No newspapers to read, no articles to pen to order, for the sake of money. No monastic obedience, no strife, in worldly ambition. Vespers on Saturday, and late mass on Sunday; from time to time a better meal at the Kozelsky tavern; to be almost ignorant of what goes on in the world. . . . There are days of exceptional distress and dejection, but it is the want of coffee in November, *of a warm new winter hat;* of the old servitors who have remained on the estate, who have to eat and whom *I cannot abandon!* . . . My conscience whispers that the Lord will forgive me and will have mercy upon me on the Day of Judgment. But the misery lies in that this rapturous Nirvana—more animal, however, than ascetic—is but a magic moment of oblivion. . . . Reality shrieks loudly: "Look, you lack what many sheep-like people possess, and you have not got and never will have seventy-five or fifty assured roubles a month. You have but a pension of forty-nine roubles which you must give away to your poor good wife and her servant girl for their support in Kozelsk; and you must rack your brains, imagine things, write and publish, in order to eat, sleep, drink, smoke, etc." ' There is a great weariness in these words. And here is another passage from a letter written to Philipov: 'The arrival of my wife in her present state of mind, of which you know, and the sudden necessity of having to go to the capital without any financial resources, have finally brought me to such a pass . . . that I cannot even think how I shall manage to eat to-morrow. Friends have been charitable all along during these last three months, some giving me ten, others twenty. I have already ceased to be ashamed.'

Financial difficulties finally obliged him to sell Kudinovo to a peasant.

This phase of his life was also marked by terrible ailments. Leontiev suffered from insomnia, megrim, diarrhoea, stomach pains, irritation of the bladder, bronchitis, chapped hands and feet, rashes and swelling. In addition he was afflicted with a disease of the spinal marrow and the contraction of the urinary canal. And finally, in 1886, he fell ill with a septic poisoning of the blood and an inflammation of the lymphatic vessels of his hand. On several occasions he was near to death. To Philipov he wrote: 'A worthy punishment for my *terrible* former life! . . . And so, after my *two last acute illnesses*, when I recovered at length from the cruel and varied torments, I was filled with such an intolerable hatred of my whole past, not only of my remote half-godless, dissolute, proud and self-satisfied past, but also of my more immediate past when I gradually saw the light of truth in Mount Athos. . . . I dare not even pray wholeheartedly for my complete recovery, for example, from my chief complaint (rashes and sores); I fear lest in my ingratitude I may, like the damned, pursue my old course!' In another letter to Gubastov he wrote that his years of service in Moscow had broken him: 'That was the hermitage.' That was where he had been 'inwardly initiated' into the invisible monasticism. Reconciliation with everything except his sins and his ardent past, indifference, an even life of prayer, but also a passionate invocation of peace and the forgiveness of sins. But Leontiev was not yet ready for the final abandonment of the world, for the monastic life; nor yet could he abide the world any longer, the world where sorrow was his only companion. And thus, poised between two worlds, he sank into a state of spiritual despondency.

II

In 1887 Leontiev retired on a pension which just enabled him to make ends meet. 'Ever since I retired', he wrote to Philipov, 'I have been in a state of blissful quietism, like a Turk who only prays, smokes and contemplates.' In the spring of that year, Leontiev sought refuge in the Optina Monastery. He remembered his vow to become a monk. And indeed, ever since he had taken that vow, he could find no real pleasure in the world. He was drawn to the monastery as to some new birthplace. He had a particular link with the Optina Monastery through his friendship with Father Clement Zederholm and the Elder Ambrose. Before he finally settled down in Optina, Leontiev had paid frequent visits to Father Zederholm, who began to exercise an important influence upon his life. Father Zederholm was the son of a German pastor and a converted Protestant. He was an educated and cultured man with whom Leontiev could discuss all the problems perplexing him. Father Zederholm was an exceptional person in the world of the Optina Monastery, into which he had come from an entirely different world. He had entered this Russian monastery, famed for its ancient traditions and elders, leaving behind him a life of worldly culture and German Lutheranism, which was spiritually so different and remote. This contrast interested and attracted Leontiev.

Father Zederholm was personally not a particularly attractive figure. He was a man of strong character, a seeker for

[116]

Divine truth, but nevertheless an average sort of person in the world and in the monastic life. Spiritually he was not fitted to be an Elder, and he could become one. Once he had been converted to the Orthodox religion, he proved to be a strict and devoted follower, like the German Lutheran that he was. But he did not feel himself completely at ease in the Orthodox faith. In his spiritual make-up there were still traits of Protestant piety and the fear of God. There was an air of moral austerity and dryness about him. There were no complications in his character; he was a more or less elementary being. Leontiev was a man of far greater stature than he was, but he needed his ecclesiastical support and encouragement. Thus, in his eyes Father Zederholm assumed a significance that was hardly in keeping with his merit. Of immeasurably greater spiritual importance for Leontiev's life was the Elder Ambrose, who was the holy man of Optina at the time. It was he, more than Father Zederholm, who was Leontiev's spiritual guide. But he finally passed under his tutelage only after Father Zederholm's death. 'When Clement died, and I was waiting to be called before Father Ambrose, I prayed before the image of the Saviour: "O Lord, move the Elder so that he may be a support and consolation. You know my struggle!" (It was very fierce at the time, for I was still capable of falling in love, and still more with myself!)'

Leontiev rented a two-storied house in the vicinity of the monastery, and it eventually became known as 'the Consulate'. With his arrival in Optina his life took on a calmer and more joyful course. But it would be a mistake to imagine that Leontiev's life in Optina at once conformed to the monastic mode. That was not the case. He brought with him his furniture, his gentlemanly habits, his tastes. We have Alexandrov's description of Leontiev's life in Optina: 'First of all he went to Optina alone and stayed for a while in the hermitage. He then moved to a small two-storied house with a garden, situated just outside the monastery walls, which he rented from the monastery until the end of his stay in Optina. He then sent for his wife and his young and trusty servants, Varya and Sasha, engaged a not too expensive cook and a boy, Petrusha, from a neighbouring village to help Varya, who already had children to look after, and Sasha, who had additional work to do in the garden, and to attend to the horse which he had bought cheaply for driving about and making occasional visits to neighbouring landlords, and settled down to a completely original sort of life, half-monastic, half-squire, yet full of a religiously moving, tender and peaceful poetry, and of the captivating beauty of an ancient patriarchal Orthodox-Russian style of life, at once lordly and generous, and wonderfully elegant and sensitive to contemporary political, social and literary trends of thought.'

I must leave Alexandrov answerable for this too idyllic picture of Leontiev's life. His description fails to correspond entirely with the tragic character of Leontiev's life. But it is true that he did live in Optina in a gentlemanly and squire-like fashion at a time when his soul was preparing for its monastic initiation. This way of living was, indeed, an essential part of his nature, his noumenal quality. In Gubastov's unpleasantly written recollections of Leontiev, in which his lack of comprehension of his friend is apparent, he asserted that Leontiev was not fitted to be a monk and that his humility was of brief duration. But that was a superficial judgment, for Leontiev was confronted with many contradictions, difficulties and temptations, to which the majority of monks were strangers. His taking of monastic vows, and his obedience, were an event of far greater specific gravity than those of simpler and more authentically integral natures. In Mount Athos and in Optina Leontiev allowed himself a certain margin of weakness and non-observance of religious requirements. He never became a real monk. Nevertheless, this innate pagan, this Turk, this quinquecento Renaissance man, this conceited Russian squire, had accomplished a real and miraculous transformation of his nature. Here is Gubastov's description of his character: 'Leontiev was a spoilt, eccentric, and despotic Russian *barin* with "impatiently complex needs", of which to his misfortune he was a lasting slave. The slightest acquaintanceship with him revealed the unmistakable traits of a Russian landowner, born and bred in the days of serfdom. His inability to do without numerous servants, his love of being surrounded by them, his patriarchal and despotic treatment of them, his attitude to country life, village amusements, all bespoke the Russian nobleman and aristocrat.' Quite characteristically he lived above his means and made debts. He was unusually disinterested and liberal, and in appearance the typical *barin* with old-world manners. He attached great importance to his being treated not only as a writer but also as a nobleman of good descent.

His stay at the Optina Monastery turned out to be one of his most productive periods as a writer. Among the works he wrote there were an interesting critical study of Leo Tolstoy, *Analysis, Style, and Tendencies*, *The Notes of a Hermit*, and *Turgeniev in Moscow*. The Elder Ambrose gave him his blessing for the continuation of his literary work. Almost everything he wrote received the Elder's blessing. Of its kind this was a unique phenomenon in the history of Russian literature. The Elders approved of Leontiev's inner spiritual development, and looked upon him as a true Orthodox Christian. Leontiev's stormy and passionately contradictory nature began to find some peace, and he retired more and more from the world. In August 1891 he took the secret monastic vows in the name of Clement. Immediately afterwards, with the blessing of the Elder Ambrose, he left Optina forever, and entered the Toritza-Sergeievsky Lavra monastery. Bidding him farewell, Father Ambrose said: 'We shall meet soon.' In these words he foretold an early death both for Leontiev and himself. Two months later Father Ambrose had died. And soon after his arrival at the Sergeievsky monastery Leontiev fell ill with pneumonia. On the 12th of November, 1891, his illness proved fatal. He was buried in the Gethsemane hermitage.

III

While in Moscow and in Optina Leontiev was in close contact with a large number of people. He had plenty of good friends. He had also his circle of admirers among the younger generation. Nevertheless he was a solitary figure, alone with his more profound thoughts, misunderstood and superfluous. On the whole he treated people better than they treated him. Those who know Leontiev exclusively by his 'fanatical' writings may judge him wrongly. He was essentially kind rather than cold or cruel, and he was very considerate in his dealings with others. His letters were disarming in their frankness and sincerity. When engaged in personal polemics he showed every delicacy and consideration. This was particularly true of his polemic with Astafiev, who had violently and crudely attacked him. Leontiev was modest rather than self-confident, although he was aware of the value of his personality and gifts. His modesty was especially evinced in the writings of his last period.

During his Moscow period he had come in contact with younger men and he liked their company. He was a good and fascinating talker and an excellent story-teller. He used to meet the younger men at Astafiev's Friday gatherings, but afterwards they came to his house. He liked people to call in the evening. But he never succeeded in forming a 'school' or movement. Kartzev, who contributed a good article to a volume *In Memory of Leontiev*, said: 'It was Leontiev's aesthetic mania that inspired him to become a reactionary; he was afraid that progress might level and destroy the peculiar character of national life. But neither Count Tolstoy nor the young Moscow undergraduates had in truth any aesthetic feeling.' In the same article he called Leontiev a 'great martyr of the idea of Beauty'. His outlook and ideas did not appeal to the conservatives, who printed him and wrote about him unwillingly. In this context, Leontiev's relations with Katkov are illuminating. Katkov was a realist, whereas Leontiev was a romantic conservative. Thus, while Katkov exercised a tremendous influence on Russian politics, Leontiev had no political influence. Katkov would say *à propos* of *Byzantinism and Slavdom* that Leontiev had got nowhere. Their relationship was complicated. Leontiev defended him as a political journalist and even suggested that a statue should be erected in his honour during his lifetime. But there was no fundamental sympathy between them, but rather an antipathy. 'Katkov personally impressed me', wrote Leontiev, 'as a shifty, false and unpleasant man.' He complained of Katkov's partiality and intolerance, his inconsiderateness and ill-will towards people. He considered Katkov to be his superior in practical matters, but his inferior in the theoretical sphere. The chief bone of contention between them was over the question of the relations between the Church and State. '*The State came first; the Church afterwards;* that apparently was Katkov's view. As if the Russian State could long survive without the constant excitation and enthusiasm of *ecclesiastical* feelings.' And *à propos* of a discussion about Katkov's 'theories' Leontiev wrote this: 'The deceased, as a man of high philosophical attainment, formerly a philosopher himself by profession, had some respect (though a somewhat aloof one) for the theories of others: he admitted the possible existence of useful and brilliant hypotheses, and of profound generalizations, but he himself had neither the time nor the inclination to think about them. . . . He was not concerned with systems and theories. He evolved something approaching a theory, it would appear, only in the last years of his life. This was the confused and nowhere clearly stated theory of the supremacy of the Russian State over the Eastern Church.' Thus Leontiev and Katkov had nothing in common. But Leontiev was kinder in his treatment of Katkov than the latter was to him.

What were Leontiev's relations with the Slavophils? Of the older Slavophils he disliked Khomyakov and did not think highly of Kireyevsky. Aksakov was hostile to Leontiev's journalistic activities. We have already seen the gulf separating Leontiev from the Slavophils in matters of national policy and the question of Russia in general. Ratchinsky, for example, felt an 'invincible disgust' for Leontiev. Astfiev attacked him so coarsely and violently over his article, *Tribal Politics as an Instrument of the World Revolution*, that Leontiev broke off relations with him. Leontiev was also little appreciated in the government circles. When Leontiev tried to get into the diplomatic service again, Prince Gortchakov was reported to have said, 'we have no need of monks.' Of the younger men who frequented him he had a certain affinity with Alexandrov, but he complained that the latter *had not interpreted him spiritually* when he described his intimate experiences. He was on good terms with Philipov, the State Controller, for they had identical views on the Greco-Bulgarian dispute. But there was no evidence that Philipov understood Leontiev's fundamental position and innermost pathos. Thus these relations were limited to a superficial identity of conservative outlook. In the eyes of Stakhov and others, Leontiev was 'far too Orthodox'. Pobiedonostzev respected Leontiev as a thinker, but held himself aloof from him. In a letter addressed to Philipov, Leontiev pithily summed up his impressions of Pobiedonostzev in this way: 'He is a very useful person. But how? Like frost, he stops further decay; but he will not help anything *to grow*. He is not only not a creator, he is not even a reactionary, not even a renovator, not even a restorer, but merely a conservative in the narrowest sense of the word; mere frost; a watchman, I say; a stuffy tomb; an "innocent" old maid, and nothing more!'

But Rozanov was Leontiev's great consolation. This remarkable writer did appreciate and highly value Leontiev's ideas and creative work. He interpreted them in a different and more profound way than had been done so far. 'The structure of Leontiev's thought at the time', said Rozanov, 'coincided to such an extent with my own, that there was no need for discussion and ultimate agreement between us: from the very first to the very last word we understood each other.' No one had interpreted or spoken of Leontiev in that way before. It was not until the twentieth century that there appeared a generation of people capable of appreciating him in a way that his contemporaries like Katkov, Aksakov, Pobiedonostzev, Ratchinsky, and others, had failed to do. There was only one point of difference between Leontiev and Rozanov: the former was an aristocrat, the latter was a democrat, 'a teacher in a provincial gymnasium.' Rozanov was indignant with Leontiev for his admiration of a character like Vronsky; but he did understand Leontiev's aestheticism and the complexity of his religious drama. There is a brilliant description of Leontiev by him, in which something of his extraordinary personality is suggested, though the portrait is not completely realized. 'A great aesthetician and politician,' Rozanov wrote in his first article about Leontiev, 'he saw in history the surging masses of peoples, loving and adoring them; but being only an aesthete and politician, he was altogether blind to the holy centre of their general movement, which invisibly guides, preserves, and supports those who are advancing. He noticed only the wandering crowds, the naturalistic herds of "human cattle", but everything he noted in this sphere was true, exact and scientific; but there is a holy image that, remaining unknown to him in its dark receptacle, has chosen these crowds, and guides them to the open temple awaiting them; and all that he so much loved in history, these blazing candles, waving banners, the smoke spiraling to heaven, all these exist not by virtue of their beauty, but by virtue of their service and their position in front of a small black icon. Out of this strange and almost pagan ecstasy emerges a third peculiarity of the writer we are studying: the excessive part played in his thought by negation at the expense of affirmation, by resentment at the expense of love, hope and impulse. The aesthetic principle is essentially passive; it encourages contemplation, it holds us back, it turns us away from everything that contradicts it; but it can never inspire us to action or sacrifice. For the sake of the earthly Aphrodite men will not embark upon crusades, they will not start revolutions, they will not shed their blood. And Leontiev truly knew and loved her alone. The Heavenly Aphrodite, man's ethical principle, is what completely moves, inspires and conquers man; for that he has shed and will never tire of shedding his blood. Leontiev had no hope of the future; and that was because, while worrying about men and fearing for them, he essentially failed to see in them the unique quality for which they could be respected,—and he did not respect them. Blind to the sources of ethical impulses, with, as it were, an atrophied taste for them, he did not love man more than he might have loved his dress and the beauty of his movements. . . . That strange passiveness to reality, which has been called his "reactionary ethos", was the authentic product of it. His appeal to men was limited to a love of such remnants of beauty as survived in life, to an attempt to piece together and cement these fragments.'

Rozanov's portrait is brilliant but not altogether correct. Therein he opposed the democratic feeling for life and history to the aristocratic one. But Leontiev was not merely an amoral aesthete, he had his own aristocratic moral attitude to life. His kindly and companionable relations with the people about him, and his friends, disproves the amoralistic interpretation of his personality. He was aware of man's individual soul, loved it and took pains with it. Both Ageyev and Bulgakov, who fortuitously shared some of their opinions about Leontiev, failed to take this fact into consideration. Zakerzhevsky, another critic, even attempted according to the fashion of the day to make him out to be a Satanist, but there was, of course, no foundation in this. Leontiev was ruthless in his political philosophy but not in life. Despite his constant poverty and want, he was always generous and ready to help his friends. He liked the responsibility of looking after people. He had his 'children of the soul', his servants Varya and Nicolas, to whose welfare he attended with touching care. His letters were full of fond solicitude for their intimate life. He sympathized with their little worries, he arranged for them to be married, he suffered with them in their troubles. He treated his servants as members of his family. Thus he showed an active love for his fellow-beings. He made glad, worried, rejoiced and grieved with them. His feeling for human joy and suffering was certainly not blunted as it would have been were he merely a degenerate aesthete. His was a passionate nature, full of compassion and consideration for individual human souls. In his treatment of his crazy wife he showed great kindness and patience, although she caused him great suffering. He preferred her to any other wife and humbly bore this trial in which he discerned a higher purpose. His wife's untidiness was a source of great anguish to his sensitive nature, and he would half-shut his eyes when he accepted a match from her and saw her dirty finger nails. Thus he remained an aesthete to the last, but the sense of religious morality was also strongly developed in him. 'I could illustrate the conflict between poetry and morality from some incidents in my own life,' he wrote to Alexandrov. 'I confess that the *former* had often a greater say, not because of a lack in me of *natural* kindness and honesty (they were both strongly ingrained in my nature), but as a result of my *exclusively aesthetic outlook on the world.* . . . And if *finally*, in my old age, I began (after the age of forty) to prefer morality to poetry, then I owed this in truth not to the passing years, my age, my illnesses, but to *Mount Athos* and, later, to the *Optina* monastery. . . . The only anti-dote for a man of wide and varied imagination against the *poetry of elegant immorality* is the *poetry of religion.*' And else-where he wrote: 'The poetry of life is enchanting while morality is, alas, too often boring and monotonous. . . . *Faith, prayer, the Church, the poetry of the Orthodox religion with all its ritual* and all the ascetic "corrective" of its spirit,—these are the only means of giving a poetic foundation to prosaic family life.' This passage reveals a very serious ethical trait in Leontiev, a tremendous spiritual labour and conflict within him. 'I, poor sinner, love all *earthly* beauty; but I have come to this, that I *can no longer* prefer it to *heavenly* beauty when I am offered a choice!'

Leontiev's moral consciousness was transcendental rather than immanent or autonomous. And he justified his trans-cendental morality on aesthetic grounds. His moral con-sciousness differed fundamentally not only from that of Kant and Tolstoy, but it was essentially non-Christian. Thus Leon-tiev represented a particular moral type, rather than an amoral one as he was popularly made out to be. But Roza-nov was right in maintaining that Leontiev was little aware of the inner psychic life of the national masses in history, that from the standpoint of his aristocratic consciousness the masses were little more than material.

There were passages in Leontiev's letters in which he complained bitterly of people, of his solitude, of the hard fate befallen him in his old age. In this context, his letters to Olga Sergeyevna Kartzev were of particular interest. In one of these letters he compared himself to a pedigree dog which had been run over by a cart. He recalled an incident of this kind he had seen in the Crimea. 'Would it not have been better to kill it? But for a believer in the after-life and in Church doctrines such a course is out of the question. On the contrary he must pray in order to live and have time to expiate his sins. He must live on, with a broken back, struggling! . . . But while we used to call specially to bring that dog a little something to eat, friends find it more difficult to look in with a morsel of *spiritual food*.' Writing to Kartzev he said: 'What business have you, and people of your age, healthy and ardent, still capable of trusting your minds, your rightness and failure, with a bruised corpse you have accidentally stumbled over. Many thanks even for writing condescendingly, another would not even have done as much. . . . In the last few years I have become so accustomed to the laziness, meanness and animal egotism of the people I have met, that I am amazed and rejoiced at any purely human treatment of me.' Leontiev had developed romantic and poetic associations with the Kartzev family. The family consisted of a mother, two sisters and a brother, who was in the diplomatic service and for whose intelligence Leontiev had a very high regard. The family lived in Petersburg, and Leontiev waxed quite soulful and lyrical when he recalled the evenings he had spent there. 'I shall never forget', he wrote to one of the sisters, 'either your friendship, your kindness, your brilliant conversational powers, your lamp, the dear and playful Andrewsha, your satin furniture, and your grey furniture studded with red buttons, your two elder tigers and their affectionate treatment of my sinful self, the harps, the cutlets, my all-night vigils in Millionnaya Street. . . . If one cherishes the remembrance of any particular spot in one's beloved village, a meadow or a flower-garden for example, then one remembers with a smile of sympathy even a rag that an old peasant woman has let drop in passing, between the violets and the roses.'

These letters reflected the intimate side of Leontiev's nature, his soul, his heart, his romantic sensibility, his longing for the beauty of life. But only a man bordering on a state of love could have written letters like these. Here is a letter he wrote to Olga Sergeyevna Kartzev from which it is clear that he dreamt of an *amitié amoureuse* and was disappointed. 'Another letter from you, O. S., and it is slightly better than the others. . . . Forgive me my disappointment. When I went to Luban in the spring I was foolish enough to have hopes of a different sort of correspondence. Imagine the foolishness of such romantic notions at my age: I thought to myself, here is a young, clever, lovely and passionate girl, a practical one into the bargain . . . and there is a weary elderly man, exhausted with struggling, but still young of mind, and with a heart capable of reviving at the sight of beauty. There is a friendship between them, a close friendship. Their relationship is irreproachable. His wants are few. He is sometimes even glad to be merely *alive*, to be able to look upon people, upon nature, to participate in some way in the exchange of minds. In his company time for her passes easily and gaily, far more gaily than when she is with the majority of those terrible and uniform young men who pay her court. They correspond, they laugh together, they speak of their worries, frankly, intelligibly and in detail, when they feel bored or sad; they discuss God, life, love even, love in general. And that goes on for years. She gets married for love or otherwise, but their poetic friendship remains unbroken. No one, not even her husband, can have a word to say against this relationship, about which there is no shadow of reproach but only the fragrance of honesty and intelligence. . . . Is it not very foolish? . . . And you write to me about the marriage of a friend of yours, which is none of my business, or that the Germans welcomed the troops better than could have been expected. By the way, I give you my word, that I am saying this for the last time. You wished simplicity, that is, frankness: well, I am being frank with you. Once and for all! I shall not write like this again; I shall write plainly, but in a different sense, that is, reticently and flatly. . . . No, Olga Sergeyevna, you are perhaps very intelligent, but there is a whole world of thought and emotion beyond your ken. Can you understand this, for example? Can you understand it well, clearly in your mind, and warmly in your heart? Can you understand me when I say that nothing comes to me *freely*? Nothing is forgiven me, as it is to many others. . . .'

Thus Leontiev's heart, his romantic longing, was still unsatisfied even in his old age. It is only too clear from their correspondence that Olga Sergeyevna Kartzev was not his ideal. His letter reflects a bitter disappointment. And so it was to prove to his dying day, for Leontiev never did meet his soul-mate, and his romantic longing was never satisfied. His niece, Marya Vladimirovna Leontiev, would appear to be the person who was most closely and intimately related to him, but we have hardly any evidence as to the nature of these relations. There was also a special friendship between him and U. S. Kartzev. In a letter to him Leontiev wrote: 'Having asked *you*, and no other, to come down and see me for a day, for a whole day in your life and mine, I abandon everything else to fate and the laws of sad human nature. . . . Only in you, my youthful and cunning tiger-poet, do I find a combination of those qualities and defects which are necessary to me for the attainment of my goal. In carrying out this undertaking, I shall have faith only in you and in your counsel. Although in dealing with you one has to be careful not to tear and gash one's hands, yet one can distil from you that precious rosy oil which no machine could press out from others. . . .'

Most of Leontiev's letters had a sad note about them. He failed to evoke from others that response he desired; he failed to discover that love for which he thirsted. He was destined to end his days without having experienced either a profound love or a deep friendship. He was to have no knowledge of the spiritual atmosphere of true sympathy and unfailing understanding. He said of himself: 'I like the work of the intelligence; but it seems to me, I like still more to be *enraptured*, to be carried away by *admiration*.' His nature exacted a warmer relationship with people, the gratification of his psychic and affective needs. On some people, the young particularly, Leontiev made an irresistible impression. One of these, I. Kolyshko, gave the following account of the impression made on him by Leontiev: 'Lean, muscular, nervous, with sparkling eyes like those of a youth, he drew attention to himself by his appearance as well as by his youthful, resonant voice and abrupt yet always graceful gestures. He did not look fifty. He was talking or, to be more correct, improvising upon a topic, I forget which. Listening to the music of his beautiful rhetoric and absorbed in his passionate utterance, I could scarce follow the transitions of his restless, lightning-like, and involved thought. It seemed independent of him, owing him no allegiance, flaming up now here, now there, and illuminating the dark distant horizons in least expected places. It was like a storm, a hurricane, overwhelming his audience. It even occurred to me that he was posing, that he was playing on his fascination, but I could not resist listening to him, just as I could not help being amazed at his tremendous power of logic, his fiery imagination, and in addition, at that peculiar quality in him which did not depend either on his mind or his rhetoric, but which was, perhaps, harder to achieve. . . . I can only describe this quality as the noble militancy of his spirit and the spectacular courage of his mind. . . .' And yet this was the man who scarcely exercised any influence upon his contemporaries! But there was another man who played a unique and important part in Leontiev's development. It was Vladimir Solovyev. Their relations necessitate a special investigation.

IV

Vladimir Solovyev was also a solitary and little understood figure, a thinker well in advance of his time. His meeting with Leontiev was the most important event in the latter's life. They differed from each other in many respects, in their mental outlook, in their education and in their peculiar psychic structure. Solovyev was a metaphysician, who had graduated in the school of German philosophy, an abstract theologian and scholastic, a gnostic with occult tendencies, an intimate poet whose verse was dedicated to heavenly love, and a political journalist, inclined to humanitarian liberalism and to a rather simplified application of Christianity to social life. Solovyev's constructions were too smoothly wrought, too rationalized, too clear. But there was something within him, less clear, unrevealed, unexpressed. He was one of the most enigmatic of Russian thinkers, no less so than Gogol, more so than Dostoievsky. The latter revealed himself in his work, with all his contradictions, his heaven and hell, his God and Satan. But Solovyev disguised rather than revealed himself in his writings. His meaning can be only unravelled from hints, from single lines here and there, from his intimate verse. We know Leontiev's mental formation: he was biologist, a natural scientist, an artist, a literary man and an aesthete. He was never a gnostic or metaphysician. In the sphere of political thought he was the author of a profound conception in which the relation of Christianity to society was posed in a complex and dualistic manner. While Solovyev expressed himself with abstract and, sometimes, deceptive clarity, concealing and disguising his innermost thought, Leontiev expressed himself concretely, with artistic clearness, revealing the whole complexity of his nature and mind. As a writer Solovyev was not an artist, and as a man he was not an aesthete. Only in his lyrics was he able to give expression to his intimate romanticism. Leontiev's was a complex, vivid and original nature, but it was in no sense an enigmatic one. He was lucid both in his good and evil, whereas

Solovyev was vague, enigmatic and often deceptive. In his interesting article, *The Relations of Constantine Leontiev and Vladimir Solovyev*, Father Joseph Foudel very rightly said: 'Leontiev was in the habit of saying in conversation or in print *more* than he really thought. This fact had its unfortunate repercussions upon his destiny, for his passion for paradoxes made him a bugbear to people who did not know him well; and his tendency *to exaggerate* in the matter of soulful confessions has created for him the *doubtful* reputation of exceptional immorality. The case of Solovyev is the exact opposite. He never said in print all that he thought or spoke of in his circle of friends.'

On examining the history of their mutual relations, we are struck by the fact that Leontiev's attitude to Solovyev was the more frank, sincere and affectionate one. Leontiev not only developed a strong affection for Solovyev, but he may be said to have fallen in love with him. Solovyev became the great passion of his life, and for his sake he would have been prepared to renounce some of his pet ideas. He exercised a tremendous influence on Leontiev, perhaps the strongest of his life. There were many aspects of Solovyev's speculation that alienated Leontiev, but he forced himself to overcome his prejudice. Leontiev himself wrote: 'I love him personally *very much*, with all my heart; I am simply attracted to him physiologically.' That was being in love. Leontiev was fascinated by Solovyev. As to the latter, he treated Leontiev with affection, and had a great esteem for him; but he was also wary and reserved, and not prone to emotional spontaneity. They both felt that they were united by some new communal anguish about Russia, that they were inaugurating some new phase of Russian thought,

[134]

although they were interpreting it in their own way. They were both solitary thinkers and dreamers, incomprehensible to their age. Writing to Father Foudel about Solovyev, Leontiev said: 'It is incontestable that he is a genius, and I myself find it difficult to resist his "fascination" (all the more because we have an affection for each other); but nevertheless we should try and resist; we must give every genius his due, but not submit to every one.'

In his turn, Solovyev showed a great esteem for Leontiev. He thought him 'wiser than Danilevsky, more original than Hertzen, and personally more religious than Dostoievsky'. He once said to Leontiev: 'I should like to print this in Aksakov's *Russ*,—we need to be more *fearless* in order that we may speak of religious *fear* rather than of love only in our day.' Later Leontiev complained that, although Solovyev had said this, he did not print it. That was the general position at the time. While Leontiev always spoke and wrote enthusiastically about Solovyev, the latter preferred to be discreet, not to write about Leontiev, and not to say what he really thought. Thus Solovyev never satisfied Leontiev's hope and dearest wish, that he would undertake a serious critical study of his work. There was also the incident, when Leontiev had asked Solovyev to deliver judgment in the course of his dispute with Astafiev over the national question. But Solovyev was reserved, and he finally declined to arbitrate. Leontiev would say bitterly that Solovyev was 'betraying' him by his silence. Solovyev did later write an article about him; but although he rated him quite highly, the article was dry and non-committal, and it did not probe very deeply into 'Leontiev's problem'. Solovyev had not his friend's capacity for 'enthusiasm'. Leontiev could exclaim: 'I had better hold my tongue for a moment while Solovyev speaks in my place, for I am "unworthy to tie his shoelaces" for him when it is a matter of religious metaphysics and the inner spirit of general ecclesiastical regulations.' Leontiev was quite free from any feeling of competition, author's vanity, or envy. That was a noble and rare trait in his character. He made up for his abrupt and inflexible attitude to ideas by his delicacy and consideration in his personal dealings with people. Solovyev, on the contrary, liked to resolve ideological extremes and contradictions, but showed himself rude and ruthless in personal polemics. His disputes with the Slavophils, with Danilevsky and with Strakhov, shocked Leontiev both by their nature and tone. They were a serious trial for his friendship with Solovyev, but his affection for him triumphed in the end. In reply to Father Foudel's question, whether he had quarrelled with Solovyev on meeting him after a prolonged period of separation, Leontiev answered: 'Not only did we not quarrel, but we kept on embracing and kissing each other. And he even more than I. He kept on exclaiming, "Oh I am so glad to see you." He promised to come and stay with me in the winter. But I have not much hope.'

In the problem of Russia's future, Solovyev exercised a great influence on Leontiev. He shattered Leontiev's faith in the possibility of an original, non-European Russian culture. Leontiev acquiesced in his sympathy for Catholicism, but he could not accept his article on *The Decay of the Medieval Spirit*. His friendship could not withstand this assault on his beliefs. He could not forgive him for establishing a connection between Christianity and both humanitarian progress and democracy. Such a contention outraged his holy of holies, the core of his religion and aesthetics. His passionate love for Solovyev turned to passionate enmity,—an enmity such as only a lover could feel. This quarrel poisoned Leontiev's last days. His break with Solovyev was the thing that worried him most on his deathbed. He did not have the strength to write a reply to Solovyev's article, to castigate this 'betrayal', this surrender to the spirit of liberal and equalitarian progress. 'My "strings", it would seem, are frayed from over-patience and from the lack of timely support. . . . I should like to take wings, but I *can not*. The *spirit* has left me. But after this I can have nothing in common with Solovyev.'

With his characteristic impulsiveness, Leontiev adumbrated a whole campaign of persecution against Solovyev, and he even proposed to get him exiled from Russia. He accused him of insincerity. In his letters he called him 'Satan' and 'rascal'. He suggested to the spiritual authorities that they should raise their voice against him. He urged the Metropolitan to deliver a sermon against the confusion of Christianity with democracy and progress. He tore up Solovyev's photograph.

There was a feeling of impotence about this clash between Leontiev and Solovyev. Solovyev troubled Leontiev as did no one else in his life. Leontiev accepted his decision in many things; and very often Solovyev was right. He insisted, for example, on the realization of Christian truth in social life. But there was a limit to Leontiev's concessions. The dispute between them was not resolved in Leontiev's lifetime. First of all Solovyev had been the stronger influence. But towards the close of Solovyev's life Leontiev's spirit began to assert its influence upon him; Leontiev's pessimistic view of earthly life and history began to bear fruit. Leontiev had also been the first to sense the coming victory of the anti-Christian spirit. First, Leontiev had been disillusioned in his ideal of an original Russian culture; then Solovyev was, in his turn, disillusioned in his ideal of a universal Christian community. They both had now reached the dark frontier of history, they stood on the edge of an abyss. And the story of their relationship is an illuminating one for us.

V

Leontiev spent the last years of his life in the discomforting knowledge that he was unsuccessful, little appreciated and of little account as a literary and ideological influence. He saw this as the enigma of his personal destiny, of his *fatum* as he called it. He interpreted it religiously and discerned an inner purpose in it. He had the sentiment that there was 'something special about his destiny'. 'To have said that I was untalented or had little talent, that I was not an "artist", would have been false and stupid on my part. It simply would not have been true. Nor have I ever heard others say it. Such a degree of humility is not Christian. . . . There were many people who could have done a great deal to make me known and famous; they apparently sympathized with and admired me; but they did very little. Was it bad faith or my unworthiness? Yes, of course it was my unworthiness, my spiritual unworthiness, my sinfulness rather than my intellectual or artistic unworthiness. God did not judge it right for me to forget myself and to forget Him: that is how I have learned to understand my destiny. Had it not been for a whole conjunction of oppressive circumstances I should, perhaps, have never turned to Him. . . . My life did not require or "need" a success of that sort, with its satisfaction and satiety. It sufficed me apparently to have a "moderate" *succès d'estime,* and it came to me when I had become more apathetic to everything. . . . And having become convinced that men's injustice in this matter was but an instrument of Divine wrath and mercy, I have long grown out of the habit of giving way to the most natural emotions of anger and bitterness against these people.' 'Perhaps people will begin speaking of me after my death; and very likely now, on earth, fame would have been of little use to me, and so God did not give it me.' He sensed a fatality in the disposition of circumstances. He noted that a certain combination of circumstances prevented the publication of articles about him. Men who had expressed a great personal liking for his work and ideas never wrote the articles they said they would about him. He had hoped that historians would confirm his theory of 'simplified confusion', but they paid no attention to him. He could not bear this indifference entirely with equanimity. He was grieved at the neglect of his ideas, and had often bitter things to say about it in his letters. 'A few good, just and even severe critical articles would have comforted me more in view of the unanimous indifference to me, than all this personal affection without any written testimony. . . . Approaching ever nearer to the last Day of Judgment, I should finally like to know whether all these labours and thoughts are worth anything or not! . . . For *my own sake,* I had need *myself* of honest and severe criticism!' And he began to be irritated with Vladimir Solovyev for 'always embracing and kissing me, and saying Oh! I am so glad to see you!' He even began to have doubts, and to think that writing was not worth while. 'What special desire can there be at my age to write merely for the sake of publication, without a strong

[139]

feeling of sympathy, without being daily *aware* of the influence I was exercising.' He wrote to Alexandrov assuming that his article, *Analysis, Style and Tendencies*, would not be printed in the form it was written: 'If not, then I make you a present of it, in memory of a man who attempted everything but who did not succeed in pleasing more than two or three people. And even so, chiefly on grounds of personal friendship!' 'In obedience to the dying wish of my great teacher, I shall henceforth write only when in *need* (financial) or because of a strong *urge* to do so, but there can be no such urge in a man of sixty, who has long been exhausted by the silent contempt of some and the unworthy betrayal of others.' This sounds very bitter for a man who was not personally egotistic and had no excessive literary ambitions. But there was a limit to the indifference he could suffer. A writer conscious of his vocation cannot bear to find himself in a desert, he cannot reconcile himself to the fact that his message falls on deaf ears. It required a new generation to appreciate and begin to understand Leontiev. Leontiev never became a professional *littérateur* but preserved his character of a *barin*. He only wrote when inspired or when he was stimulated by outside events. But his *fatum*, the neglect and lack of appreciation with which he was surrounded, weakened his inspiration. By way of a literary destiny, Leontiev's was typical of a solitary, original thinker following a path away from the main roads, with their 'camps' and 'tendencies'. The influence he exercised must be considered in another light from that exercised by writers like Katkov and Aksakov. But Vladimir Solovyev's was a parallel case, for he was appreciated and valued only for his articles on the national problems, which were not the main preoccupation of his life.

Leontiev's attitude to Russian literature and Russian writers is a matter of great interest. He was a fine and, for his time, an original critic, who had little in common with the majority critics who had long dictated to Russian literature. Leontiev was more concerned with the aesthetic aspect of life than with that of art. For an aesthete he wrote very little about art and literature: it is clear from his creative work and life, that he did not seek essentially an escape in art and literature from the ugliness of life. When he was disgusted with life, he took refuge in a monastery rather than in art. In his search of beauty he had for a long time confined himself to the sphere of politics and history, although he had met with only bitter disappointments in his quest. He has himself confessed that he was more at home in the political than in the aesthetic sphere; for him 'the State had more value than two or three superfluous literary stars'. With his accustomed daring he even ventured to suggest that 'in our confused, irritating and spiritless epoch, types such as Vronsky are much more useful to us than great novelists', in other words, more useful than Tolstoy himself. He was in search of life as opposed to 'reflected life'. He failed to grasp the living significance of art.

His outstanding critical work was a study of Tolstoy's novels, entitled, *Analysis, Style and Tendencies*. It is a subtle, though somewhat old-fashioned essay from the standpoint of style. But for its time it was an original and quite remarkable piece of work. It was an age of utilitarian principles in criticism, an age which disregarded the autonomous value of literature. In the 1860's Leontiev had already championed the autonomy of art and beauty, and had insisted upon the rights of aesthetic criticism. In his *Letter of a Provincial to Turgeniev*, written in 1860, he had already said: 'If there is no true beauty in creation,—and beauty is itself a fact, the highest of natural phenomena,—then creation must be lower than any mediocre scientific fact, lower than any superficial record.' In his earliest critical essays Leontiev realized the possibility of a formal aesthetic criticism. He found the moral, social and utilitarian type of criticism repugnant to his nature; but the generation of the 1860's, 1870's and 1880's was definitely prejudiced against the aesthetic form of criticism. Leontiev was thus a precursor of the new literary generation of the 1890's, which did admit the cult of Beauty for its own sake. His *Analysis, Style and Tendencies* was the first and only attempt of its kind to examine Tolstoy's novels from the standpoint of analytical, formal and aesthetic criticism. Leontiev esteemed Tolstoy very highly as a novelist, and he had a particular liking for *Anna Karenina*. He was delighted that Tolstoy had taken 'the initiative to re-establish the aesthetic rights of higher society'. He had great sympathy for the characters of Vronsky and Prince Andrew as representing virile and aristocratic types capable of serving the State. He cleverly analysed the lack of correspondence between *War and Peace* and the actual history of the age it portrayed; and his preference went out to *Anna Karenina* as the more artistically perfect work. He also believed that Pushkin had reflected more faithfully the 'tendencies' of that age. 'To obtain the maximum degree of aesthetic pleasure, an exacting critic must not only take account of the *events*, but also of the *omni-psychic music* accompanying them; he must estimate the *tendencies* of the age.' In Leontiev's day such terms as

[142]

'omni-psychic music' had not been heard of before. Far in advance of his age, he had already expressed the mood of the coming 1890's and 1900's. He was responsible for other such apt definitions as: 'Language, or, as it was formerly called, *style*, or again, to put it in another way, the manner of expression, is an outward thing, but in literature it is synonymous with a man's person and manners: it is the *most visible* outward expression of the *innermost* and sacred life of the spirit. Men's personality and manners mirror the unconscious far more than the conscious: a man's nature or developed character is stronger than his intelligence.' Thus Leontiev propounded a subjective approach to aesthetic criticism. As he put it, 'Aesthetic criticism, like a sincere religious debate, must inevitably begin with a living *personal* emotion and only later attempt to justify and affirm it logically. . . . Therein the personal *faith* comes first, and the general affirmation afterwards; the *subjective taste* precedes the explanation.' Not everyone can set up to be a critic; an aesthetic criticism requires an aesthetic disposition, an aesthetic sensibility. But with the exception of Bielinsky most Russian critics were devoid of any aesthetic taste.

Leontiev's aesthetic sensibility was, on the whole, more European than Russian. His enthusiasm for the East was also in a sense European. Here we are confronted with what might appear to be an enigmatic aspect of Leontiev's nature. He was not particularly fond of Russian literature, he did not value it so highly, he did not admire its style. There was much in it that shocked him, and impressed him as being anti-aesthetic. 'I still think that in some ways our school is simply *intolerable*, even in the works of its greatest representatives. *It is particularly intolerable in that aspect of it which may*

[143]

be called in special cases simply "*language*" and, in others, *generally its external manner or* "*style*".' He was alienated by the partiality of Russian writers for deformity and their dislike of the beautiful aspects of life. 'Our writers are simply afraid to deal with those aspects of reality which are ideal, graceful and beautiful. That, they say, is not Russian, not the Russian manner! The painters invariably choose a drunken subject, some sickly, ugly-faced, poor and coarse creature out of our Russian life. The Russian artist is afraid to paint a handsome priest, a venerable monk. No, he feels happier when he depicts a drunken clergyman or a coarse fanatical monk. The boys and girls must all be snub-nosed, dirty and scrofulous; the peasant women cowed and beaten; the civil servants, rogues; the general, a dolt, and so forth. That is what they call the *Russian type*.'

Leontiev was disgusted with the *negative* tendency in Russian literature which he discerned among some of the greatest writers beginning with Gogol. He failed to appreciate the essential humanity of this literature. He was irritated and alienated both by the moral tone and the naturalist method of the Russian writers. He accused Tolstoy of being an exponent of naturalism, while he called himself an 'aesthetic monoman, an artistic psychopath'. He could not bear coarseness or vulgarity in artistic works. Nor did he approve of the propensity displayed by Russian writers for psychological analysis. 'I am bored to death with this all-Russian "scratch yourself" habit. . . . And I am, of course, a disciple of the same school, but I protest at least, rather than accept its tenets unconditionally.' Expressiveness and vividness were the two qualities he judged valuable in an artist. He was in ecstasies over 'Pushkin's varied, sensitive, demoniac and splendid genius'. His tastes were those of a Renaissance man, and Russian literature impressed him as being gloomy and oppressive, joyless and non-Renaissance. He also grieved at the decay of the Russian literary style. He lovingly recalled the old artists, particularly the European ones. 'I find that the ancient narrative manner is more *real* in the best sense of the term, in other words, it is more truthful and more authentic according to the fundamental laws of our spirit.' He would have liked to break out of the frame of the Russian literary school. 'The majority of us', he wrote to Alexandrov, 'are still unable to emerge from the frame :

GOGOL

TURGENIEV   DOSTOIEVSKY

TOLSTOY

But I wish to smash it!' 'It is necessary, even though for a short while, to shake off the yoke of the Gogolian school from which even Leo Tolstoy was unable to free himself. . . . Try and get hold of George Sand's *Lucrèce Floriani*. It is a model of simplicity. It is not of course at all Christian; but then the Venus of Milo was not a Madonna, but yet beautiful.'

Leontiev liked the flower of pagan art; and he had an aesthetic love for everything breathing the spirit of the Renaissance. The Christianity he loved was exclusively monastic and ascetic. Russian literature was full of moral Christian motifs which, in his opinion, reflected neither a real flowering culture nor a real religious Christian life. Thus his choice lay between the Venus of Milo, the Renaissance, and

Pushkin, on the one hand, and Mount Athos, the Optina Monastery, and the Elder Ambrose, on the other. Nevertheless he had a higher appreciation of Turgeniev than many of his contemporaries; he also liked Tolstoy, although he discerned a taint in him; he also admitted the qualities of Pissemsky and overrated Markevitch. But he definitely disliked Gogol as the source of the decadence that was creeping into Russian literature; and he did not at all appreciate Dostoievsky. And those were his limitations and defects as a critic.

In Leontiev's opinion, Gogol was the original instigator of the naturalist and negative tendency in Russian literature. But this was a fundamental error which he shared with many others. He failed to understand the nature of Gogol's creative work, which appeared to him essentially deformed and hostile to beauty. His antipathy went so far, that, in his youth, he had never wished to meet Gogol personally. 'For various reasons I felt an almost personal enmity towards him. Among others, for his *Dead Souls* or, rather, for the overwhelming and hopelessly prosaic impression which that "poem" produced on me. . . . I was filled with that ineradicable living aesthetic feeling, which set a higher value on the *poetry of real life than on the artistic perfection of its literary reflections!*' Leontiev loved not only the idea of beauty but also beautiful things; and the deformities and monstrosities of Gogol's imagination revolted him. He failed to sense the strange and enigmatic character of Gogol's work, which was to inspire later such remarkable phenomena of contemporary literature as the writings of Andrei Biely. Gogol was also the source of both Sologub and Remizov. But Leontiev was perturbed and alienated by the fact that 'Gogol had the appearance of a surly waiter, or that *not a single woman* in his writings resembles a living character; his women are either old, like Korobotchka and Pulcheria Ivanovna, or mere shadows, like Annuntziata and Oksana; a sort of pictorial reflection of *beautiful flesh* but without any *soul*'. At this point Leontiev did sense the underlying anguish of Gogol's work, but he did not know how to define this feeling; he could not grasp the essence of the plot, namely, that in Gogol man's complete organic image had already been disintegrated. Thus Gogol was a fantasist, who saw monsters rather than men, but not at all a realist. There is a certain affinity between certain aspects of his work and those of Picasso's cubist period. Nevertheless, he remains one of the most perfect of Russian artists, attaining a high degree of beauty in his portrayal of evil and deformity. This aspect of his genius escaped Leontiev's more old-fashioned critical and aesthetic judgment.

Leontiev's negative and hostile attitude to Dostoievsky was even more disappointing. He wrote to Alexandrov as follows about him: 'I do not find it easy to praise him: I cannot bear his "monstrous" novels, although I am aware of their qualities.' On the face of it, Leontiev should have felt a certain sympathy for Dostoievsky, because, like him, he had a tragic vision of life and a complex religious problem to solve. But he spoke of Dostoievsky in such an unworthy way, that it is difficult to forgive him. '*War and Peace* has, at least, performed this great service, that its tragic outlook is sane and sober, rather than ugly and deformed, as it is with many of our writers. It is not the same thing as Dostoievsky's tragedy, enacted in doss-houses, brothels and almost in the Preobrazhensky hospital. The tragic vision of *War and*

Peace is useful because it inspires heroism and patriotic feeling; but Dostoievsky's vision can, perhaps, only excite a few psychopaths, living in badly furnished rooms.' We can sense in these unpleasant words, spoken by one of the most remarkable Russian thinkers about the greatest Russian genius, a pointless aristocratic squeamishness and superficial aestheticism, which are only an obstacle in the way of probing spiritual depths. In this instance, the superficial aesthete got the upper hand of Leontiev, the psychologist. He was alienated by the elements of vulgarity and distortion in Dostoievsky's work, by the lack in it of grace and beauty or, rather, picturesqueness. He sensed in him the democrat and philanthropist; and that was the one unforgivable sin as far as Leontiev was concerned. In the scale of values, he situated Dostoievsky well below Tolstoy, and he was quite prepared to overrate not only Pissemsky but also Markievitch in comparison to him. Thus he relegated Dostoievsky's work to the category of non-beautiful, and made no effort to penetrate its mystery. He could not forgive Dostoievsky aesthetically for his 'psychopathic' heroes. It did not occur to him that Dostoievsky had discovered an entirely new and hitherto unknown source of beauty. 'I value Dostoievsky incomparably higher as a political journalist and a moralist than as a novelist. His *Journal of an Author*—with all due respect for the admirers of the late novelist—is a hundred times more precious to me than his novels.'

Those were, indeed, the limitations of Leontiev's spiritual nature. Beyond this barrier his consciousness seemed unable to penetrate. We shall have to be satisfied with tracing the origin of his prejudiced judgment of Dostoievsky. His aesthetic and religious formation shut him off from Dostoiev-

[148]

sky's infinite world and all his great spiritual revelations. Aesthetically a man of the Renaissance, a lover of beauty and picturesqueness, of life and plenitude, Leontiev, the aristocrat, recoiled instinctively from that disintegration and dissolution of the soul in which all sense of form is lost. His religious formation was austere and founded upon Byzantine Orthodoxy; he was attracted by monastic asceticism: he was a pessimist who had rejected all earthly hopes. It was not surprising then that he had some difficulty in appreciating Dostoievsky. 'Only those who are little familiar with true Orthodoxy, with the Christianity of the Holy Fathers and the Elders of Mount Athos and Optina, can judge *The Brothers Karamazov* to be an Orthodox novel.' Leontiev, who was on intimate terms with the Elder Ambrose, definitely asserted that the Elder Zossima was a figment of Dostoievsky's imagination and in no sense an Orthodox type. Indeed, he reacted violently against Dostoievsky's 'pink' Christianity. He ascribed its origin to the author's philanthropic and humanistic inclinations, and judged him to have little experience in religious matters. 'Dostoievsky's subjectivity may have deluded him into imagining that he was portraying for us, in *The Brothers Karamazov*, real types of Russian Orthodoxy and monasticism. His own dreams of a *heavenly* Jerusalem on *this earth* were of more account to him than the living truth or the authentic character of the Church.'

And in fact, Leontiev was right: the Elder Zossima had spiritually little in common with the Elder Ambrose. But then, the whole of Dostoievsky's creative work was prophetic rather than realistic in temper, whereas Leontiev was a stranger to the prophetic spirit. He carried his negation of

Dostoievsky as a religious psychologist so far, that he preferred Zola to him: 'The work of Zola (in *La Faute de l'Abbé Mouret*) approximates more nearly to the spirit of authentic personal monasticism than the superficial and sentimental make-believe of *The Brothers Karamazov*.' Its prophetic religiosity was a closed book to Leontiev; but he was right in his contention that Dostoievsky did not portray real Russian Orthodox types, the traditional types of Orthodox monasticism, but created a new type.

Leontiev had the intention of writing a novel about his conversion, but the idea never took shape. 'I wish that many other educated men may be inspired to believe, on reading how I was converted from an aesthete and pantheist, a dissolute one into the bargain, and an incredibly sensual one too, into a Christian believer, and how after that I, poor sinner, struggled fiercely for many years, until the Lord brought peace to my soul and soothed my once truly Satanic fantasy.' That novel would have portrayed the traditional religious psychology,—the quest of personal salvation. But in portraying the quest of a new earth and a new heaven, of a new humanity, Dostoievsky gave birth to a new religious consciousness.

For all his sensibility and love of beauty, Leontiev's aesthetic taste was not irreproachable. He lacked the real refinement of Western aesthetes, their high degree of aesthetic culture. Thus his reading was not particularly choice. But his greatest lapse from good taste was, perhaps, his predilection for the style of the age of Alexander III,—a style which was not only the acme of bad taste but was also symptomatic of the decay of the older beauty and the collapse of the Russian monarchy. The productions of that age were outstanding for their lack of taste and ugliness. The spirit of that reign was without any sense of beauty. Thus Leontiev's critical taste did sometimes betray him. His enthusiastic praise of Markievitch was an example of this. We may even suspect that he praised Markievitch as a novelist because he approved of his conservative attitude. But that is much the same as praising an artist for his 'progressive' outlook. There was a want of taste, too, in the 'Russian get-up' or peasant smock which he flaunted as an aesthetic protest against the drab attire of Western Europe.

Very characteristic of Leontiev's aesthetic attitude was the article he published in *Russkaya Misl,* an article entitled 'Some Reminiscences and Reflections about the Late A. Grigoriev'. Grigoriev was a remarkable and little known Russian critic. In Leontiev's eyes, he was obsessed with the same passionate quest of life as he was himself. Grigoriev held aloof from the Slavophils, who treated him with suspicion. He was the mouthpiece of a different aspect of Russian life,—that of the riot of passion and the senses. And Leontiev was obviously more in sympathy with Grigoriev than with the well-meaning domestic tenets of the Slavophils. According to him the poetry of debauch and love of women was rooted in the depths of the Russian consciousness. This aspect of his thought, as well as his sympathetic attitude to Europe's past, attracted Leontiev far more than the social virtues of the Slavophils. It is true, he was more attached to the Church and Orthodoxy than the Slavophils, but this attachment was strictly monastic and ascetic in spirit. Leontiev, like Grigoriev, feared impersonality more than vice. Thus Leontiev lacked all the virtues of the Slavophils, their steadiness, their academic turn of mind, their social solidity and earnestness.

He was an effervescent character; he advised Alexandrov not to take up a professorial appointment, because that would have been incompatible with poetry. When Alexandrov contracted a marriage with a woman of a somewhat lower rank, Leontiev never ceased giving him, in his letters, aesthetic advice, and was anxious that his wife should be *comme il faut*. Leontiev was both a poet of life and a monk, and life held no other perspective for him. Outside poetry and monasticism he had no other love or desire. He has described his joy of life in a letter to E. S. Kartzev in these words: 'I shall soon, at last, be at home in my dear village, where even the cocks dare not crow loudly when I am writing, where my niece makes a detour of my quarters, for fear of disturbing my poetic mood by some aspect of her bearing which may strike me as ungraceful at that moment, and thus slightly upset my contemplative bliss. . . . Again the greenery in my courtyard, again the century-old elm trees by the pond; again the thirteen-year-old Vara in her pretty sarafan, bringing me excellent coffee, as I want it, on a Japanese tray, and everything is where I want it. . . . Again Vespers at home on Saturdays. . . . And the rustle of those incomparable thickets, and the reeds, and the field flowers, and the talks with the Elders of Optina.' In this descriptive passage we see Leontiev as he really was.

CHAPTER V

THE MISSION OF RUSSIA AND OF SLAVDOM.
THE ORIGINAL TYPE OF CULTURE. A
CRITIQUE OF NATIONALISM. BYZAN-
TINISM. LEONTIEV LOSES FAITH IN THE
DESTINY OF THE RUSSIAN PEOPLE. PRO-
PHECIES ABOUT THE RUSSIAN REVOLU-
TION.

I

The problem of Russia, that of her destiny and vocation, was the main theme of Leontiev's speculation, and a constant source of anxiety to him. He elaborated an original doctrine in no way resembling that of the Slavophils or that of the Westerners. But with time his views of Russia's future were considerably modified. His early optimism,— for he never lacked hope or illusion,—later gave way to disillusion, and he died in a state bordering on despair. He was not afraid of looking truth in the face; and he was strong enough to renounce the dream of his life. He made a clean sweep of all his hopes, of all his fine illusions. He was by nature a daring, highly disinterested and unfettered thinker. Although facts compelled him to modify his judgments, he nevertheless remained faithful to his principle. He had formulated a new and singular doctrine of nationality, a doctrine which is worth closer examination. He was in no sense a nationalist as might appear at first sight: he was even

[153]

avowedly hostile to nationalism. The principle of race and blood had no intrinsic value for him. He was very much on his guard against it. Like Solovyev he tended to be a universalist. What mattered in the first place were the universal elements, dominating the national idea and stimulating national development. It followed that the decay and ruin of a nation was caused by the disintegration of these universal elements. Rome was Solovyev's universal symbol, Byzantium was Leontiev's. The latter had, indeed, never believed in Russia or its people, but rather in the principles of the Byzantine Church and State. The only mission he believed in was the universal Byzantine one. Byzantinism was in no sense a national mission. In this connection, Leontiev was not at all a particularist. When considering the organizing and morphological influence of the universal Byzantine principle apart, he looked on the Russian people in no favourable light, expecting little of any significance or good from it; he had a deep-seated distrust of the 'demotic' element, looking upon it as brute matter, which should not be shaped by the masses themselves but by a universal principle or great idea. In Leontiev's mind, the essential fact was *not the people itself, but the idea dominating it*. He exalted the Church and the State above the nation. This interpretation of the problem was not exactly that of a Slavophil. 'I do not understand the French. They do not care *what France* they love or serve.... For my part I should like my country to be worthy of my esteem. It would require coercion to oblige me to support *any Russia*.' He already envisaged the possibility of a Russia that he would not wish to love, that he could not love,—that of a liberal, democratic and atheist Russia. *Thus he attached more importance to the idea than to*

Russia itself. In this respect, he had a certain affinity with Solovyev, but their ideas were fundamentally different. Both Leontiev and Solovyev lived in an age when the traditions, which had formed the older Slavophil thinkers, were being discarded. Leontiev's conception of popular traditions was aesthetic rather than realistic; and his aestheticism was ample proof of his decadence by the standards of the older Slavophils. Thus, his philosophy was one of despair, while that of the Slavophils had an optimistic element about it. Similarly, his outlook on Europe was fundamentally opposed to that of the Slavophil school. He did not at all believe that the essential sources of European history and culture (Catholicism and Feudalism) had as their foundation those false and corrupting principles which have reduced Europe to a lower historic and cultural level. Despite his Byzantinism he did not think that only a civilization founded upon Greek Orthodoxy could be a true and superior civilization, and that a culture founded upon Catholicism must necessarily be a false and inferior one. He never attacked the European aristocratic formula or its traditions of chivalry as did the Slavophils. But he did hate modern, liberal and equalitarian Europe, the triumph of the *petit bourgeois* spirit: 'As long as Europe will have dynasties, as long as it will have some sense of order, as long as the vestiges of its great Christian and classical ages will not be supplanted by an uncouth and atheistic workers' Republic, which alone is capable of uniting the West *for even a short while*, we need have no excessive fear of her and should regard her worthy of our esteem and friendship.' He valued the East and Russia chiefly because they stood in the way of the triumph of democracy and bourgeois atheism: 'Should the West lapse

[155]

into a state of anarchy, we shall have need of all our discipline to help her, to save that which is worthy of saving, that which has made her great,—the Church, no matter which, the State, the remnants of poetry, and perhaps even science itself, the tendentious brand of science, but that which is austere and sad!' In this statement there is no trace of nationalism: Leontiev refused to subscribe to the usual Slavophil interpretation of Western history. He ridiculed the Slavophil criticism of the separation of powers in the West, of conquest as the basis of medieval authority, and of the rationalization of the Church. 'It is doubtful whether the great works of the ancient West could have been produced without an independent Church, without a chivalrous aristocracy, without the struggle between powerful castes, and without the charters which were the outcome of these struggles. It is easy enough to imitate the contemporary West, discounting all these feudal and Roman "evils". Ruin can be brought about without the help of Popes, chivalry or charters. It may be brought about even quicker and more effectively without the experience of such mighty and real forces of the past. . . . Let us be on our guard! Let us not rejoice at having lacked the experience of political dualism; on the contrary, let us regret the fact that our Church is too dependent upon the secular power.'

Leontiev's historical outlook was much more objective and impartial, and in certain respects far more just, than that of the Slavophils, who distorted history for the benefit of their national pride and prejudice. The historical thesis of the Slavophil school will not bear serious examination. Leontiev's views, on the other hand, were the outcome of his aesthetic, religious and philosophical outlook, rather than of a particular historical theory. His political ideas were much more independent than those of the Slavophils. In the same way, his interpretation of Russian history was strongly opposed to the Slavophil conception. He loved and highly appreciated Peter the Great. According to him, the reigns of Peter the Great and Catherine II were far more representative of 'the complex flowering' of Russian culture in a multiplicity of forms than the Muscovite age. It was then that Russia underwent a process of Europeanization, a process which in no wise displeased him. On the contrary, he attributed to it a positive value: 'Prior to the reign of Peter the Great there was a greater uniformity in our national and social life, a greater homogeneity in the parts. With the advent of Peter the Great, we may observe a marked differentiation in our society, a greater diversity without which, indeed, there is no creativeness among peoples. It only needed Catherine to bring these forces to a head, to allow for leisure, taste, intellectual creativeness, and loftier sentiments in social life. The despotism of Peter the Great was essentially liberal and aristocratic. Catherine's liberalism was similar in character. Her great merit was to have assisted the flowering, the creativeness and the growth of Russia. By bestowing privileges on the nobility, she increased inequality; and by giving less emphasis to the bureaucratic function of the nobility, she exalted the aristocratic virtues of race and personality.'

Such ideas were essentially Western rather than Slavophil. There was not the least trace of Byzantine mysticism in Leontiev's appreciation of Peter the Great and Catherine. We must add, that Leontiev founded his idea of Tsarism on a positive rather than a mystical basis. Although his religious conscience was monastic and ascetic, he attributed no mystical foundation to the temporal theocratic kingdom. His cult of Tsarist authority was pagan in character: the notion of theocracy did not appeal to him as it did to Solovyev. He regarded the mystical consecration of Tsarism as an historic fact pertaining to the natural order of things. He attached no mystical aspiration to it, but only the earthly hope of a flowering of culture in its most diverse forms. In contradistinction to the Slavophils, he approved highly of the policy of Nicolas I, interpreting it in terms of a State policy rather than of a national one. In the controversy which arose between Nicolas I and the Slavophils, he sided wholeheartedly with the Tsar, whom he believed to be more clear-sighted than his opponents. He judged that Nicolas I knew what he was doing, whereas the Slavophils were only hastening the process of decay and death by adopting the liberal and democratic programme. His reign marked the end of the period of development and progress; the 'complex flowering' had reached its limit. An age of 'simplifying confusion' was now at hand. Hence the reactionary elements were justified in reasserting their rights. Whereas Catherine had still been creative, the Emperor Nicolas I could do no more than preserve what had been achieved in order to prevent 'the confusion of that which had been so markedly differentiated thanks to historical progress'. Leontiev was ready enough to admit that the Slavophils had some justification in their attitude to the Church. They wished to see it more powerful and more free, although 'they vitiated this legitimate aspiration by *nationalist* passions'. But in matters of State and national policy Nicolas I was all-powerful. In the following passage Leontiev described his attitude towards the Slavophils: 'It (the Slavophil doctrine) impressed me as being too liberal and equalitarian to be able to defend us effectively against the modern West. But that is only one aspect of the question. Another thing which made me distrust their doctrine was their unilateral morality. In my eyes their doctrine was neither aesthetic nor political. Katkov's views on the problem of the State gave me much greater satisfaction. . . . In the sphere of historical and abstract aestheticism, I felt that I had much more in common with Herzen than with the contemporary Slavophils. On reading only Khomyakov and Aksakov it would not occur to anyone to hate the world bourgeoisie (towards which the *worker* of the West is also tending); Herzen was content *simply to despise this human type*, which evolution tends to generalize and which is immeasurably disappointing.' The texture of Leontiev's being was different from that of the Slavophils, his cellular disposition was quite distinct from theirs. He regarded the principle of the Russian State as being more essentially Russian than the social and popular principle. 'Although our ancient systems of government have, from the time of Peter the Great onwards, adopted many Western features, we may nevertheless affirm that the principle of the Russian State is more original than that of a free rural community.' This is the antithesis of the Slavophil conception. The Slavophils believed that the State principle introduced by Peter the Great had disfigured the life of the Russian people. Leontiev differed from the Slavophils as much as he did from Dostoievsky in that he had no great passion for the people. *He believed in the Church, in ideas, in beauty, in certain elect, powerful and creative personalities; but he had no faith in the people, in the human mass.* And this fact made him an original figure in

Russian literature, for our thinkers usually founded great hopes in the people; they had faith in the people even when they had lost faith in everything else. Populism is fundamentally a Russian movement, which dominated our *intelligentsia* throughout the nineteenth century. The fact that Leontiev was not a populist, and that he criticized the foundations of the movement was perhaps the most outstanding feature about him as a writer. We do not imply that he was necessarily right, for populism had in it an element of truth in relation to our national genius. And in the context of the Russian idea as such, Khomyakov will always hold his own against that Prussian martinet, Nicolas I.

II

Leontiev could not very well be a populist, for he was an aristocrat by instinct and conviction,—a rare phenomenon in Russian thought. To begin with, he entertained some traditional Slavophil illusions, but he discarded them later for good and all. His article, *Education and Populism*, was, however, written in this vein. His thought had not yet matured and grown independent; it was still in the thrall of that tradition which tended to idealize the common people, the peasantry. But Leontiev forthwith attempted to draw a distinction between 'the people' and 'the peasantry'. He defended the illiteracy, the 'barbarity', of the peasantry as a source of national originality. He expressed the fear that education might stifle this originality. Such a view had nothing populist about it; it was rather the opinion of an aristocrat and aesthete. 'It is not a question of being an equal of the *moujik*. It is not even necessary to be loved by him in all things or to love him. But we should love him within the *national and aesthetic framework*. We should love him for his *style*.' Thus Leontiev appears to have interpreted the peasantry aesthetically, loving their *popular style* but not the peasantry itself. He was completely free from any moral bias in the matter. He was prepared to idealize a *moujik* simply because he was the opposite of a bourgeois. He liked humble village churches, country monasteries, thatched huts, ploughing peasants. He was attracted by this picturesque and popular aspect of life in the Balkans and in Turkey as well as in Russia. He wished to preserve its local colour and flavour,—everything that stood in the way of the destructive elements. He idealized the rural community in a conventional way, as a conservative principle checking the growth of the proletariat. But that was only a secondary aspect of his theory of Russia and her future development. The fundamental principles of his theory were far from populist. *He had discovered that the principle of national autonomy was in itself a democratic principle, the consequences of which implied revolutionary action;* and that this had prepared the way for the triumph of the progressive ideas of liberalism and equality, which in their turn undermined national originality. He pointed out the inner contradiction implicit in the principle of nationality, a contradiction which hastens its destruction. Leontiev's propositions were extreme, biased and original. But for all their errors, they were unusually interesting. To do him justice, he was the first to pose the problem clearly. His remarkable article, *Racial Policy as an Instrument of World Revolution*, aroused indignation in conservative and nationalist circles. There was a brusque retort from Astafiev, who called him an enemy of the national ideal. Aksakov likewise looked upon him as an opponent of Slavophil ideas.

Leontiev's aristocratic attitude encouraged him to see truth and beauty in the universal and organizing principles of the Church and the State, in objective ideas, that is, rather than in the popular genius or in the principle of nationality as an independent value. According to him, the truth and beauty of the Russian people was manifest not in the genius of the masses, but in the Byzantine order, which had organized and moulded this genius in its image. The Byzantine principles were aristocratic ones imposed from above, while racial principles were essentially democratic and came from below. Russia owed whatever greatness and originality she possessed to the conservative virtues of Byzantine Orthodoxy and autocracy, rather than to that national cement which has been termed 'the autonomous will of the people'. In fact, the objective sum of political and religious ideas was the foundation that made Russia an impressive and independent world of her own, an Eastern world confronting the Western world. The free reign of popular principles, of national autonomy, untrammelled by any superior or external control could only lead to the ruin and disintegration of Russia. And in fact the strength and unity of Russia were destroyed by the ebullience of popular and national elements; but the Revolution was followed by an attempt on the part of the Russian State to re-organize itself on the basis of popular activity. Leontiev failed to understand or to appreciate the importance of popular currents in the process of national development. He did not believe in the Russian people or in any other people. According to him a great nation survived and prospered by virtue of the coercive idea dominating its foundation, rather than by virtue of any autonomous force. Leontiev made a ruthless analysis of the principle underlying national autonomy. 'The purely racial idea has nothing creative about it, but is merely a particular aspect of the universal idea of equality and abstract universal happiness. The equality of persons and classes, the equality of peoples and countries, the breaking down of all barriers, the violent overthrow or the peaceful sapping of all religions, of all secular or caste authority; all these are the manifestations of the same principle. It matters little what disguise it assumes —the pretentious extravaganzas of Parisian demagogy or the provincial aspirations of a small people eager to acquire equality of political rights.' 'A truly national policy should uphold, even beyond its frontiers, the *spiritual principles* of its racial history, power and glory, rather than the *crude* idea of race. The policy of the Orthodox spirit should have pre-eminence over that of the Slav body, over that of propaganda in favour of Bulgar "flesh". . . . As to the national idea, when it is *divorced from religion*, it is merely the resurrection of the idea of 1789,—the beginning of equality and general freedom,—wearing *the mask of pseudo-nationality*. The national principle, without a religious foundation, is identical with the principle of equality and liberalism, which is *a slow but sure dissolvent*.' 'The liberal national myth has *deceived* everyone. It has deceived the most experienced and the most intelligent men. It represents nothing more than *the revolution in disguise*. It is one of the most subtle and false *metamorphoses* of the democratic Proteus, of that process of liberation and levelling from below which, since the end of the last century, has been persistently undermining by every means at its disposal the grandiose edifice of the Germano-

Roman State.' 'The men who, in the nineteenth century, seek to emancipate their fellow-men or to establish nationality, have national objectives in view. But when they have attained their political ends, it becomes clear that they have only succeeded in founding a hybrid organism, that is, a product which increasingly eliminates the national aspect of culture and tradition, and which increasingly favours the fusion of these liberated peoples, or of peoples who have become freely assimilated with other races or nations in order to reduce them to the general type of progressive European bourgeoisie. Universal democracy and political nationalism are but two different aspects of the same thing.'

Leontiev denied the intrinsic value of the national principle. 'What was a nation or race, when stripped of its system of religious and political ideas? Why should it be loved for its own sake? For its purity of blood? And what is pure blood? Spiritual sterility! All the great nations are of mixed blood! Is language a reason? . . . It is true that language is a precious instrument which helps us to formulate the ideas and sentiments we cherish. It is a false sentiment to love the race for its own sake. It is different, of course, if the race reflects our particular ideas, our deeper feelings. . . . The *equality of nations* is synonymous with universal equality and freedom, a useful and agreeable thing for all, a sum of general happiness, a state of anarchy or the boredom of universal peace. The idea of nationalities founded upon race, as manifest in the nineteenth century, is a purely liberal, anti-political and anti-religious one. It has great destructive potentialities, but nothing constructive to offer in return. It has no *cultural* criterion, for culture implies diversity.'

Thus Leontiev was inclined to take an unfavourable view

[164]

of the Slav policy in the East. He disliked the principles of Slavdom, the importation of nationalistic principles into the East of Europe. He valued Byzantine ecclesiastical and political principles as the only true constructive ones. Hence the sympathy he felt for the Greeks and even the Turks. 'After her emancipation, united Italy lost something of her originality. She fell into line with France, and all the other European countries. We witnessed the profanation of her spiritual and plastic images, which the true intelligent Europe used to admire so enthusiastically.' 'After achieving her unity, Germany has shown a perceptible decline in her national culture.' Her character becomes commonplace and less individual. Autonomy and national emancipation tend to de-personalize her and to produce a levelling from below.' It is worth pondering on this paradox which is in direct contradiction to current ideas: 'When nationalism was less inspired by nationalist ideas than by the interests of religion, of the aristocracy and the monarchy, then *it incarnated itself unconsciously.* Whole nations and individual men displayed the most varied characteristics, and flourished upon them. Now that nationalism seeks *to emancipate itself, to become composite, to group men together less in the name of distinct interests* such as religion, monarchy, and privileged classes, than in the name of equality, freedom, and race for its own sake,—now an essentially identical result is achieved, in brief, democracy. All nations and all men begin to look alike, more and more so. Thus their spiritual misery grows ever more acute. The flowering of culture is brought about by transcendental principles and the objective value of ideas. In itself the principle of nationality has one content. It is essentially democratic, and hence capable only of "deflowering".' 'The national principle in its crude state, stripped of particular religious *forms*, and presented, as it is to-day, in its purely racial aspect, is a *falsehood*. Racial policy is one of the strangest *illusions* of the nineteenth century. In the strict sense of the word, *there is nothing national in the racial principle.*'

Leontiev prophesied that national autonomy and emancipation would cause the Balkan peoples to lose their national physiognomy, to become the victims of European liberalism and equality, of the bourgeois and vulgar democratic spirit. In the Near East, too, Orthodoxy would be bound to suffer. Leontiev ridiculed the lofty dreams of the older Slavophils, for whom the emancipation of the Slavs went hand in hand with the flowering of the Orthodox idea and of Pan-Slavism. 'When living in Turkey, I very quickly learnt a bitter truth: I was horrified and saddened to discover that the strength of certain Slav and Orthodox elements in the East was due entirely to the Turks. I began to suspect that, for want of anything better, the Mussulman tyranny could, in spite of its viciousness, be a source of strength for our Slav characteristics, that without its consolidating pressure, the dissolving influence of Europeanism would become still more troublesome.' In the idea of expelling the Turks he saw the working of a European, democratic and liberal tendency, which had nothing in common with Russian or Slav policy. But he also insisted that 'Russia's mission never was or ever will be a purely Slav one. Nor could it well be, for until the present time the Slavs have lacked any purely Slav qualities. . . . Russia herself has long ceased to be an essentially Slav power'. He gave priority to the interests of Orthodoxy in the East over those of the Slavs. He even went so far as to say: 'An Orthodox bishop, were he a most cruel and vicious character, were he even a baptized Mongol or of any other race, should have more value in our eyes than twenty Slav demagogues and progressivists.'

Leontiev believed that Constantinople could only be either Russian or Turkish. In the hands of the Slavs it would become a revolutionary centre. The war of 1877 did not appeal to him, because it was fought for the cause of Slav liberation rather than for that of religious belief. He looked upon Pan-Slavism as a danger for Russia. '*The Russian and Orthodox idea of culture* is an original, noble and austere one. It has all the value of a State religion. Pan-Slavism *at any price* is largely a derivative idea. It is a modern *liberal and unifying* ideal, a striving after *uniformity*. It is at bottom the product of the European revolutionary trend.' Leontiev regarded the spread of Pan-Slavism in the East as the triumph of a vulgar democratic principle. He accused the Slavophils of being too eager to bring about a levelling of classes and to claim equality of civic rights, in a word, of furthering the process of democratization against which he had already often inveighed. As we have observed, Leontiev tended to be a Turkophil rather than a Slavophil. For the same reason, he admired the Germans for their greater consciousness of those principles which helped to keep alive the traditions of the old Europe he loved. They were less inclined to be deluded by the false democratic ideals of liberty and equality. He was particularly incensed against France as a democratic Republic and hotbed of universal revolution. But he did not love Germany and the German people for themselves. Indeed, he was far more in debt to French influence and culture than to German. He was more at home with the Latin spirit. But he

[167]

loved and respected the Monarchy and also the warlike instinct which had lost none of their force in Germany. Thus he was in favour of a Russo-German *entente*, while at the same time being aware of the possibilities of a war with Germany. He used to argue that 'either a firm alliance or a war between the two countries would be equally popular with our people'. In these words there was a certain contempt for the people; but as it happened, later events were to justify him. He further believed that the growth and consolidation of Germany would work out to Russia's advantage, even if it was achieved at Russia's expense. In that he was, indeed, a thinker of exceptional temerity. But how did Leontiev reconcile his original interpretation of nationality with Russia and her people, with Russia's mission in the world? In order to help the reader to understand this, we shall first of all have to analyse Leontiev's conception of Byzantinism.

III

In Leontiev's opinion, Russia owed her strength and greatness to her Byzantine rather than to her national Slav principles. And her whole future depended upon her faithfulness to the Byzantine traditions. What is Byzantinism? Leontiev placed a high value on Byzantine culture at a time when historians were apt to neglect, under-estimate, or treat it with contempt. Leontiev, on the contrary, could say, 'Slavdom as a whole is still a sphinx, an enigma; but the abstract idea of Byzantinism is extremely clear and comprehensible.' Slavdom, as he saw it, was something 'amorphous, elemental, unorganized, not unlike the formation of distant and spacious clouds out of which the most varied forms might emerge'. 'As distinct from this, when we think of Byzantium, we behold the clear and austere plan of a spacious and capacious edifice. We know that Byzantinism stands for autocracy in government. In religion, it implies a certain definite type of Christianity, which is distinct from that of the West with its heresies and schisms. In the ethical sphere, as we know, the Byzantine ideal often falls short of that lofty and, in many cases, exaggerated conception of man's earthly personality, which is the historical outcome of German feudalism; its tendency is rather to stress man's disillusionment with all earthly manifestations, with earthly happiness, with the constancy of our own purity, with our ability to lead the perfect terrestrial life. We know that Byzantinism (like Christianity in general) repudiates all hope of a universal happiness for all peoples, that it is the exact antithesis of the idea of a universal humanity in the sense of terrestrial equality, universal freedom, universal perfection, and universal contentment.'

Leontiev, moreover, discovered the aesthetic beauties of Byzantium. In his day this was a new and original discovery. But he was attracted less by the refinements of a decadent culture, of that late Hellenism which had become so inextricably interwoven with ascetic Christianity, than by its strong organizing and authoritarian principles of Church and State. He did not reflect sufficiently upon the causes of Byzantium's decline, upon its internal disease. Vladimir Solovyev, on the other hand, attempted to give a religious explanation of the inevitable collapse of the Byzantine Empire. But Leontiev pointed to the fact that Byzantinism was transplanted to Russia, where it exercised a greater influence than in the West. 'In its contacts with Russia, in

[169]

the fifteenth century and later, Byzantinism found a poor, empty and undeveloped country. Thus it could not be as deeply modified in Russia as it was in the West, and it penetrated our national life in its general outlines in a much purer form.' It did not strike Leontiev, however, that this union of Byzantine principles and Russian rudimentary life was comparable to marriage between an old man and a young girl, a rarely successful experiment. But it is true that Byzantinism did help in the internal as well as the external organization of Russia. 'What would Russian Christianity be without its Byzantine *foundations* and *forms?*' Leontiev inquired. There was a tendency on the part of Russian elemental paganism to disrupt Christian forms and to overthrow Christian foundations, as was apparent in popular mystical sectarianism. The unity of the Church was cemented by Byzantinism. 'There are only three mighty forces in Russia: Byzantine Orthodoxy, our native and unlimited autocracy and, perhaps, our agricultural community. . . . Our Tsarism, which is so fruitful and conservative, has grown strong thanks to the influence of Orthodoxy, of Byzantine ideas and culture. Byzantine ideas and sentiments have knitted a half-savage Russia into one unified body. . . . If we remain faithful to it, we shall be strong enough to resist the pressure of "international" Europe, should she ever attempt, after destroying her own noble foundations, to impose upon us her corrupt and rotten laws of petty, earthly, universal bliss and universal vulgarity!' Leontiev was very right and clear-sighted, when he stressed the importance of Byzantine principles as a conservative and cementing element in the structure of Russia. But he failed to foresee that Russian internationalism would prove even stronger and more insistent than that of Europe.

On this point his outlook was subject to inner contradictions. Towards the end of his life his forebodings about Russia's future grew stronger. In his *Byzantinism and Slavdom* we already find this passage: 'In the West *the conservative spirit of the higher strata of society* was always stronger than with us, and for that reason the explosions were more audible; our *conservative spirit* is weaker. Our society is, on the whole, disposed to follow others; and who knows, perhaps more rapidly!' This would seem to imply that the Byzantine principles had not really become an organic part of the Russian people, that they were artificially imposed upon it. The West, on the contrary, had its own organic principles. Leontiev noted the noble conservative principles of France, but failed to detect any such principles among the Slavs. Here we come up against the fundamental contradiction which was inherent in the whole of Leontiev's speculation about Russia, and which assumed a tragic aspect towards the end of his life. Byzantinism was alien to the spirit of the Russian people, and that accounted for the gulf between the people and the governing classes. The Russian people had apparently failed as yet to evolve an organic form of government for itself.

For a long time Leontiev believed and hoped that Russia was destined to save the crumbling and dying Europe, and to present the world with a new and loftier type of flourishing, complex and varied culture. 'Russia is not simply a State; she is a whole world of peculiar life, a specific form of government, *which has not as yet evolved an original style of cultured State for itself*. Russia is the great East; she must produce an extraordinarily original Eastern civilization in opposition to the bourgeois West.' 'I believed then,' he wrote in one of his later articles on Pan-Slavism, 'and I believe now, that, were Russia to put herself at the head of some new Oriental State, she would give the world a *new culture,* a new Slav-Oriental civilization, in place of the declining Romano-German European civilization. I was even then an eager disciple of our very remarkable and still isolated thinker, Danilevsky.' Leontiev's dependence on Danilevsky's theories, and on those of less original Slavophils, may, indeed, account for the obvious contradictions in his own thought. 'We Russians *must absolutely get off the European rails and, blazing a new trail for ourselves, we must ultimately direct the mental and social life of mankind.*' He aimed at 'the development of a peculiar, original, Slav-Asiatic civilization, as distinct from the European as the Hellenic-Roman civilization was distinct from the preceding Egyptian, Chaldean and Persian civilizations; or as distinct as the Byzantine was from the Hellenic-Roman; or again, as distinct as the *late* Romano-German civilization was from the Hellenic-Roman and the Byzantine civilizations, which preceded it and *which it partly assimilated and organically transformed.*' 'The turning point for us Russians will be the taking of Constantinople and the foundation there of a new cultural and governmental edifice.' 'Constantinople is the authentic centre to which all Christian nations should converge, *being destined sooner or later to form an Eastern-Orthodox Federation with Russia at its head.*'

The influence of Danilevsky is very marked in this passage. Leontiev had not yet found his own feet, although his originality also made itself felt. Russia's mission was to save old Europe. Her immediate task was to consolidate 'her integrity and strength, in expectation of the great and terrible hour when she should employ them in the service of the best and noblest principles of European life, in the service of that great and old Europe to which we are so indebted and which it would be well to repay in kind.' This was a universalist rather than a particularist and nationalist interpretation of Russia's mission. Leontiev's love of Europe and of her great culture was implicit in these words. It was essential for the success of this mission, that 'Russia should become as distinct from Western Europe as the Greco-Roman world was from the Asiatic and African civilizations of ancient history'. 'The people that develops its national characteristics most completely is performing the greatest service for universal civilization.' 'There are only too many indications that we Russians shall somehow alter the course of universal history, even though it be for *a short while!*' 'A people can give birth to a creative genius only when it is endowed with the most varied fundamental characteristics, and is at the same time as fundamentally distinct as possible from other peoples. And our great and magnificent All-Russian Ocean is like that!' And he advised the Russians to be not only 'a great State' but also 'a great nation'. Europe had already given much and was exhausted. The future lay with Russia, and also, perhaps, with the Greco-Slav world and with Turkey. Salvation would come from Asia. If the Russians did not undertake the creation of an original culture, then that would become the task of 'millions of other Asiatics'. Thus Leontiev presented Russians with great world problems. What foundation was there for the belief that Russia could fulfil her mission? What did Leontiev think of the Russian people?

As it turned out, Leontiev despised not only the Bulgars and the Serbs, but also the Russian people. He believed exclusively in the Byzantine idea. He attached no particular value to the Russian people, or to the Russian idea, when compared to Byzantine Orthodoxy and autocracy. He loved the aristocratic principle in whatever form it might be manifest. In a certain sense, it would be true to call Leontiev an 'internationalist' rather than a nationalist. In any case, his nationalism was too peculiarly his own. He loved the ancient rather than the contemporary Russia. 'I dislike *terribly present-day* Russia. I am not sure whether it is worth while dying for her or in her service! I love the Russia of Tsars, monks and priests; the Russia of red shirts and blue *sarafans;* the Russia of the Kremlin, of by-roads, and benign despotism.' Thus he loved only the picturesque aspects of Russia, those aspects which had been created by the coercive agency of certain ideas. 'May God preserve the majority of Russians from ever reaching the stage at which many Frenchmen have laboriously arrived, that is, *of being able to serve and love any France!* . . . What good is non-autocratic and non-Orthodox Russia to us?' Then he asked himself: 'O Lord, am I a patriot? Do I despise or honour my country? I am afraid to say. It seems to me that I love her as would a mother and at the same time despise her like a low drunken wench.'

Leontiev loved Russia in a special way quite unlike that of the Slavophils and our traditional nationalists. This love did not prevent him from uttering the bitterest and most ruthless truths about Russia and her people, truths which might have made one despair and lose all hope of Russia ever being able to accomplish her great mission. 'Our youth, I say it not without bitterness, is *dubious.* We have lived long, but have *spiritually created very little*, and now we are on the brink of a terrifying abyss.' These words might have been spoken by

[174]

Chaadayev. There were in Leontiev many such ruthless and bitter passages reminiscent of Chaadayev. 'Our Russian psychic constitution is also remarkable for this, that so far, it would appear, there has never been in history a people *less creatively gifted than we are*. The Turks, perhaps. Actually our psychic temperaments are quite original, but *we have never been able to create anything really original or astonishingly typical*. True, we have founded a *great State;* but it lacks almost any vestige of an *original governmental principle*. It has no such original and exemplary political institutions as had pagan Rome, Byzantium, old Monarchical France and Great Britain.'

Unlike the Slavophils he denied the originality of Russian autocracy. He became increasingly scathing in his criticism of Russia and her people. He was more merciless in his denunciation of the national self-delusion than more superficial critics. According to him, the sources of Russia's strength were foreign rather than native. 'We must have faith in the further development of Byzantine Christianity, in the fruitfulness of the *Turanian* strain in our blood, and also, partly, in the Orthodox *inter-susceptio* of the hard and potent German blood.' 'The Russian discipline, which is not characteristic of any other Slavs, is nothing but the product of the combined influence of principles fundamentally alien to the Slavs,—of Byzantine, Tartar and German principles. This fact is, perhaps, *very regrettable* for Slav vanity, but there it is: the discipline of our Church is completely Byzantine; the Germans still teach us order; and, as we all know, there is a great deal of Tartar blood in the veins of the Russian nobility which has for so long stood at the head of the nation. . . . Who knows, but for *these influences*, perhaps, the

Pan-Slavonic tribe, and partly the Russian people, would pass more easily than any other people or nation from their stormy lawless state into a state of *peaceful impotence*, into a state of *legal and organized anarchy*.'

Leontiev had no faith in *Russian principles*, and he did not rely upon them for his dream of Russia's universal mission. But he did believe in a *despotic idea,* capable of holding together and directing the national aspirations. This helps to explain his political reactionary views. He was a reactionary because he did not believe in the capacities of the Russian people, and because he perceived that Russia was entering upon a period of 'simplifying confusion' or, in other words, a period of disintegration. Although he was an ardent champion of the original cultural ideal, he failed to detect any original Russian thought, and was only aware of 'the Russian horror of any real independence of mind'. 'Everything great and durable in the life of the Russian people was elaborated *almost artificially, and more or less forcibly,* on the initiative of the government.' Independent initiative on the part of the people or of society, brought nothing but destruction in its wake. He did not share the Slavophil faith in the Russian earth and the Russian agricultural community. He only believed in principles coming from above. 'For the Russian people to become truly a "godly" one, it is necessary for it to be *confined, held down, paternally and conscientiously constrained.* It must not be deprived of its *external limitations and curbs,* which have for so long affirmed and inculcated *humility* and *obedience* in it. These qualities constituted its psychic character, and have made of it a truly great and exemplary people.' In the face of the democratic Slavophils, Leontiev believed that the power of the Tsars, which, in his opinion, held Russia together, developed at the same time as inequality and differentiation. And it acted as a check upon the process of simplifying confusion. 'True Russian thought should be both progressive and conservative, or more precisely, it should *develop in a reactionary manner;* that is, it should advocate an advance at certain points of historical life, but not otherwise than by means of *strong authority* and of preparedness for any sort of *coercion.*' It was Leontiev's conviction, a traditional populist one it is true, that Russia should take upon herself to initiate economic reforms and thus anticipate the impending social revolution. His grave doubts about the Russian people and his fatal premonitions of an imminent disintegration made him exclaim: 'We must *freeze* Russia to prevent her from rotting.' But this was no way to create a new, flourishing and original culture, to fulfil a positive mission in the world. 'Thank God, we are now trying to congeal our history a little bit, in the hope that it may be possible later on to take a different turning. And then let the tempestuous and rumbling train of the West speed past us into the inevitable abyss of social anarchy.' These were the words of a despairing conservative, without any faith in and hope of a complex flowering of culture or a universal mission. Leontiev was never given to mystical Messianism; his doctrine of Russia's mission was based upon an analysis of the naturalistic process going on in the country.

Leontiev had so little faith in the vitality of the purely Russian elements, that he took up a negative attitude to the Russification of outlying lands. He called this process 'a fluid, pale and levelling Europeanization'. 'The Russification of the outlying parts is nothing but a form of democratic Europeanization.' 'For our, thank God, *still variegated* State such diverse localities have their use; different religions are useful too; thank God, that this *present* process of Russification is being checked. This check is useful *indirectly;* thus Catholicism is the chief prop of Polish aspirations, let us say, but it is at the same time one of the best weapons against general indifference and atheism.' On this point Leontiev definitely parted company not only with Katkov but also with the Slavophils and the traditional conservatives. He even went so far as to maintain that peoples of other persuasions were better than the Russians. 'It is all very well to convert Uniats to Orthodoxy, but is it not more essential to think how we can *illumine our own* men of Moscow, Kaluga, Pskov, the inhabitants of Northern Palmira? Despite the confirmed non-believers of the outlying parts, Russia waxed ever stronger since the days of the Moscow Tsars; but in the hands of the Great Russian Europeans she has, within half a century, arrived at *what?* . . . We can see *what* she has arrived at now! . . . Among other things, she has reached a point, when the Old Believer, the Catholic priest, the Tartar Mullah and the most savage of the Tcherkess, have become better and less harmful to us than *our own brothers in blood and in faith (in name only, not spiritually).*' 'Russians are not made for freedom,' he wrote to Zamoriev. 'Without fear and coercion they will let everything turn to dust.' 'Can one do or affirm anything in Russia without compulsion of the severest kind? Where lies our strength? In the army, the monasteries, the officialdom and, perhaps, the peasant community. In fact, *in all that has compulsion behind it.*' 'Out of affection for Russia, I often think that all our mean personal defects are very useful from the cultural standpoint, for they *create the necessity of despotism, of inequality* and of forceful spiritual and physical discipline. These defects make us un- suited for that bourgeois and liberal civilization which is still so strongly entrenched in Europe. We are inferior to the Europeans in both our *racial* and *moral* qualities; but just as we must admit, without wishing to exaggerate our youth, that we are nevertheless *at least one century* younger than Europe, so a less gifted and less noble race may *for a period* become better from the cultural standpoint than older but more gifted races.'

Such was the straw at which Leontiev clutched in his hope for the future of Russia. In his eyes the European peoples were more gifted than the Russian people. 'Yes, my dear friend,' he wrote to Alexandrov, 'I fail to discover in Rus- sians that special and unheard of "morality" and "love", which your underground prophet, Dostoievsky, preached and which others are preaching after him, and on whose *cultural* (!) significance they depend.' Leontiev even denied that there was any original quality in Russian religiosity. 'Byzantine religious culture has in general produced all those principal *types* of Saintliness, which have later served as examples to Russians. . . . All our Saints were only the dis- ciples, the imitators and the followers of Byzantine Saints.' He boldly suggested that Russians should 'renounce the cult of Karatayev and that of the common people, too reminis- cent in their *style* of the Slavophil cult of the 1840's and 1860's'. He saw no originality in Russian Orthodoxy; he had no conception of the radiant Christianity of St. Seraphim,— the Christianity of the Resurrection.

Leontiev's judgment of Russia was in many respects similar to that of Chaadayev. They were both bitter, gloomy, pessimistic, fearless and profound; they were also both opposed to Slavophil ideas. But whereas Leontiev turned to Byzantine principles, Chaadayev pinned his hope in Western Catholic principles. Both affirmed the primacy of an objective idea over the national element, and both exalted the religious idea above the national one. Leontiev did not believe that a State could survive without mystical foundations. '*Personal morality* and even personal valour have in themselves no organizing or governmental principle. The organizing quality is not the outcome of a personal virtue or of a subjective feeling of honour, but of *external and objective* ideas, of which *religion* is the principal one.' Leontiev detected no true religious temper in the Russian nobility. As to the *intelligentsia* there was hardly any need to consider it. 'They will not shut the Churches and the monasteries yet,' he wrote to O. S. Kartzev, 'I think the laws will still allow the Russians to pray for another twenty years.' These words were, indeed, the echo of an ominous foreboding which was realized in our day. 'A man who *believes sincerely* should not have to hesitate between his faith and his country. *His faith must come first,* and his country should be sacrificed if only for this reason, that every earthly State is but a transitory phenomenon, while *my soul and the soul of my fellow-beings are eternal, and the Church is also eternal.* The Church is eternal in this sense, that if three thousand people, or three hundred people, or even *three people in all,* remained faithful to the Church on *the day when the whole of mankind on this planet was to perish,*—then these three thousand, these three hundred, these three people, will *alone be right,* and *God will be with them, while the remaining millions will be mistaken.*' 'Faith in Christ, in the Apostles and in the sacredness of the Oecumenical Councils, does not necessitate unfailing faith in Russia. The Church has lived long without Russia, and if Russia became unworthy, then the *Eternal* Church would find new and better sons for itself.'

Leontiev was not guilty of Church nationalism as were the Slavophils and Dostoievsky. In this respect his attitude was nearer to Catholicism than to Russian Orthodoxy. It was not surprising, therefore, that he was drawn within the orbit of Solovyev's influence. Leontiev differed from the Slavophils on yet another point with regard to the Russian people: he maintained that the racial and family instincts were not strongly developed among Russians, and that their attachment to the State was greater. 'The racial instinct, which is so strongly developed in Western aristocratic society, has only found expression in our Monarchy. . . . With us the principle of the State has always been stronger, more deeprooted, more developed, than either the aristocratic or the family principle. I confess that I fail to understand those who talk of the family instincts of our people. . . . All other peoples, be they German, English, Little Russian, Greek, Bulgarian, Serb, even rural or provincial Frenchmen, even Turks, have all a greater sense of the family than we, Great Russians.' Leontiev was right in his judgment: the State and Monarchical principles were developed in Russia at the expense of the aristocratic and family ones. But in another respect Leontiev shared the delusions of the Slavophils and the populists. He believed that the mission of the Slavs was to destroy free individualism, that the personalist principle should be prevented from developing in Russia and that a higher type of culture would be the result. This also accounted for his detestation of the legal principle. Although he had very rightly drawn attention to the original type of collectivism peculiar to the Russian national character, we must also point out the fundamental defect in his social philosophy. In the case of Russia, he confused primitive simplicity with flowering complexity. This Russian 'collectivism', this imperfect growth of the personalist principle, was an obstacle in the way of the development of Russian culture, an unwillingness to submit to the natural law of a passage from a simple to a complex state. Leontiev himself maintained that the development of the personality was related to a stage of 'flowering complexity'; and he was an ardent admirer of strong and full-bodied personalities. From his naturalistic standpoint, it would have been hopelessly contradictory to expect from Russia an age of flowering complexity, a cultural Renaissance as he understood it. He had no spiritual faith in the Russian people, and that was his misfortune. Everything conspired to make him doubt in the future of his country; and this disillusionment in Russia embittered his last days. In this connection, his meeting with Vladimir Solovyev proved to be of paramount importance to him.

IV

Solovyev's scepticism had the effect of gradually undermining the foundations of Leontiev's conception of Russia. 'I am doubtful about the duration of Russia's future; the *goal* of her future and her *ideal* are enigmatic. Am I the only one to think so? Certainly not! I know a number of people who are of the same opinion. But they will not commit themselves openly, they only talk about it in whispers.' 'I confess that my hopes as to Russia's cultural future have been shaken more and more.' 'It is very possible that Danil-evsky's belief in an original Russo-Slav culture on a quad-ruple foundation has no real basis. And very possibly my *former* hopes were so much smoke.' 'I do not say that I alto-gether despair of Russia's *particular* mission, but I am begin-ning to have my doubts about it.' As a last resort he con-sidered making a distinction between the religious Orthodox and the racial-Slav problem, and suggested concentrating on the former. 'For all my desire to think as I used to do—on the lines of Danilevsky—I am beginning to doubt more and more. I keep thinking of Vladimir Solovyev's bitter and almost derisive words, "Russian civilization is European". What if he is right in *this matter?* Solovyev sees things in a truer perspective; perhaps we are blinded by our desire to see things in a rosy light? . . . It is problematic whether there will ever be an entirely new, independent, complete and original culture on this earth! Even supposing the advent, later, of one or two types of new culture, we have not the right to hope that that type will be the product of an already senile Russia and of her Slav brethren, who are partly being transformed from swineherds into Europeanized liberal bourgeois!'

Leontiev attempted to resolve this contradiction in the following fashion: 'It is one thing *to believe* in an ideal and *to hope* for its realization. But it is another thing *to love* that ideal. One may love a sick and dying mother. It is the same with Russian culture: one may ardently wish for its re-covery, without having much hope of its survival.' Thus, under the disquieting influence of Solovyev, Leontiev de-parted further and further from the position of Danilevsky and the Slavophils. 'In 1882 or 1884 I met a man to whom I

[183]

made for the first time in thirty years some concessions. I did not do so out of any personal and practical considerations but *because my absolute faith in the ideal which I had shared with Danilevsky was shaken for the first time.*' 'Solovyev is the first and only man who has succeeded in troubling my mature spirit, who has forced me to alter the trend of my thoughts. . . . *He has not shaken my personal and inner faith in the spiritual truth of the Eastern Church, which is essential to the salvation of my soul after death.* But in the course of these last two or three years he has, I confess, *destroyed my hope in Russian culture.* Since then I am by way of thinking as he does, though grudgingly and despite myself, that Russia's vocation is perhaps only a religious one.'

As we shall see later, this religious vocation had its own limitations, but not the sort imposed by Dostoievsky or even Solovyev. He continued to believe,—and he could not feel otherwise,—that the Orthodox Church was the only way of salvation for his soul. It was the triumph of the ascetic and monastic theme. If Solovyev was right in the beginning, Leontiev proved more perspicacious in the end. He had a presentiment of the consequences following 'the liberal and equalitarian process', a presentiment that Solovyev did not share. Leontiev's sure instinct, his far-sightedness towards the end of his life, were truly extraordinary. He proved a better judge than other Russian thinkers of the true character of the Russian people and of the various currents which were in the process of formation in Russia. Thus he was fundamentally wiser than the Slavophils and the Westerners, Dostoievsky and Solovyev, Katkov and Aksakov. He foresaw the catastrophe out of which the new epoch was to be born. 'Petersburg Russia,' he wrote in 1880, 'that *modern* and bourgeois Europe, is creaking in all its joints. One has only to listen carefully to hear it. It is truly a sinister omen.'

There was nothing of the die-hard conservative about Leontiev. He foresaw the coming crisis, the agony of the past, and the birth of a new world. He had a clearer and better vision than others of the early rumours of Revolution. He understood the danger; and, terror-stricken by his own foreboding, he exclaimed: 'Russian society, which is already equalitarian in its customs, will be dragged more rapidly than other societies along the fatal road of general confusion. And who knows but that, like the Jews who unexpectedly gave birth to the teacher of a *new faith, we too shall unexpectedly give rise to Antichrist—sprung from the bowels of our political system, which will first of all abolish class distinctions, and then all vestiges of an ecclesiastical principle*.' A prophecy such as this was terrifying, and full of menace for the spiritual future of Russia. It was imbued, moreover, with a profound truth, and contained a warning of hidden danger. It marked the end of the history of Russian messianic hopes and expectations. And, in truth, Russia and the Russian people offered a suitable soil for the appearance of the Antichrist. In Leontiev there were completely concrete images of the Russian Revolution. He has described with amazing precision the nature of the catastrophe. In this he was a real prophet, and he mingled his forebodings with plans of action to forestall the cataclysm. Unfortunately his projects were too naïve to have any practical value.

Leontiev held liberalism in contempt as a moderate movement, which had no independence of its own and which only helped to prepare the ground for the triumph of destructive principles. He was sceptical about the possibility of a liberal regime in Russia, a country given to extremes. According to him Liberalism was '*a superficial doctrine which might easily be crushed between two non-liberal forces*, such as the mad surge of Nihilism, on the one hand, and the bold and resolute defenders of our great historical principles, on the other'. In this context Leontiev was particularly lucid. He was personally hostile to any moderate solution for Russia; the idea was aesthetically repugnant to him. He loved extremes; he believed that violent action and reaction were less dangerous than the effects of slow poison. 'No popular revolt, no new Pugatchev, could do as much harm to Russia as a pacific and lawful democratic constitution.'

Leontiev's wish came true: a 'Pugatchev revolt' did triumph over a 'lawful and pacific constitution'. This experience was, however, to prove very costly for Russia. Leontiev, like a true prophet, had foreseen that the Russian people would not be satisfied with a moderate constitutional reform, that it would plunge headlong into extremes. 'If liberalism were a little more widespread, it would bring about an explosion, and the so-called *constitution* would be the surest way of putting us under a Socialist yoke, of inciting the poorer classes to fight the rich, the landowners, the bankers and the merchants. It would be a new and even more terrible "Pugatchev revolt"! It is surprising that well-meaning men should wish to see the Tsar's power limited in the hope of pacifying Russia! With us a man of the people is governed far more by the feeling he has for the person of the Sovereign (anointed by the Lord), and by the secular habit of obeying the officers of that Sovereign, than by any natural virtues or a vague respect for legal fictions. It is well known that Russia is impervious to common sense. It is naturally

[186]

inclined to extremes. *Thus, if the power of the Monarchy were to lose its absolute significance; and if the people were to grasp that it was no longer ruled by a Sovereign, but by deputies elected according to a system of voting they did not understand (less even than the workers of other countries); then this people would reach the stage of believing that it had outgrown obedience.* At this very moment, the people is weeping in the Churches for its assassinated Emperor. It believes that its tears are *salutary for the soul*. Not only would it not weep for its elected deputies, but it would claim *as much soil and wealth as possible*, and the minimum of taxes. . . . It would certainly not fight for the freedom of the press or for Parliamentary debates.'

Leontiev's prediction has been realized. It defined the very character of the Russian Revolution some thirty-five years before it materialized. Leontiev had a much clearer vision of the real situation than other contemporary thinkers, publicists and politicians. As an aesthete he had little sympathy with jurisprudence and the law, and he tended to exalt the lawless elements of the Russian temperament. Leontiev understood very well that the world was threatened by Socialism and all its accompanying dangers. He was aware of the important problem implicit in Socialism. He therefore elaborated a method of defence intended to protect Russia against the menace. 'It is no small undertaking to teach our people the *spirit of the laws;* it might well take a century to do so. Unfortunately, great events will not wait to see the outcome. And besides, our people loves and understands authority better than laws. In its eyes a military leader is not only a more familiar but also a more sympathetic figure than a paragraph of the civil code. A constitution, which would undermine Russian authority, would not have time to teach

[187]

the people a *devotion such as the English have for their legislature*. And our people is right. I can see no other practical solution of the contemporary problem of capital and labour except in a well-established monarchical system, sanctified by the Church and limited only by its conscience. We should forge ahead of Europe in the labour question and show her an example. What in the eyes of the West is the genius of destruction should become with us a creative work. . . . *Our people has greater need of affirmations of faith and of an assured material life than of jurisprudence and true science. . . .* Only that which will satisfy both the material and the religious wants of the Russian people, can rescue the future peasant generations from the claws of the Nihilist Minotaur. Otherwise we shall fail to crush the Revolution, *and the triumph of Socialism will be assured sooner or later. It will not be a harmless and healthy triumph, the outcome of a whole progressive system, but one steeped in blood and the horrors of anarchy. . . . We must keep up with events, we must understand that a readjustment of relations between capital and labour, in all its aspects, is an ineluctable historical fact.* Do not let us deceive ourselves by turning our backs on the danger. Let us look it well in the face and, without any panic, admit that it is inevitable.'

Leontiev's insight into this great social problem was remarkable, but his proposed remedies were naïve and utopian. His desire to see Russia 'forging ahead' of Europe in the matter of solving the labour question had a Slavophil flavour about it. He clutched despairingly at a sort of hybrid conservative and monarchist Socialism. He was not satisfied, of course, with dreams like other conservatives of the time of Alexander III, who lived in an age of decency and pacifist illusions. Leontiev felt the earth burning under his feet. He heard the echo of sinister subterranean rumblings. A year before he died, he described once again, in a letter to Alexandrov, his project for a mystical and monarchical Socialism. He did not believe himself that his project could be realized: 'It happens that I see a Russian Tsar take the head of the Russian movement, and organize it somewhat after the manner in which the Emperor Constantine organized Christianity. But what is "organization" if not "*compulsion, a form of prudently established despotism, of legalized, cleverly engineered violence at the expense of the citizens' personal freedom?*" We must also bear in mind that it is most improbable that this new and complex serfdom could be organized and made to endure without a *mysticism*. If, after the annexation of Constantinople, an *extraordinary concentration* of Orthodox ecclesiastical bureaucracy, in the form of the Patriarchate and the Councils, could coincide with the development of that mystical current, which is growing in Russia, on the one hand; and with that inevitability, which is represented by the development of the labour movement, on the other; then, I am convinced, that the dual political and economic basis of the State could be preserved for a long time to come. Besides, sooner or later everything will end in a definitive *fusion*. Humanity has without doubt greatly aged.'

Leontiev could see no profound truth in Socialism. It held no attraction for him as it did for the majority of the *intelligentsia*. In his eyes Socialism was nothing more than the fatal instrument of 'simplifying confusion'. If he entertained the unrealizable dream of a mystical and monarchical Socialism, he did so in the hope of preserving some vestiges of the ancient noble culture, and to maintain in some form or other the inequality of classes, and the aristocratic idea. Towards the end of his life, when speaking of the Slavs, he employed a sinister enough image: 'They will evaporate like a soap-bubble. They will be swallowed up a little after the other races in the bosom of the detestable Western bourgeoisie; they will end by being trampled upon—and that will be a good thing—by a Chinese invasion.' Incidentally, we may note that the religion of Confucius is a religion of almost *pure morality*, and has no knowledge of a personal God. Buddhism, which is also very powerful in China, is quite simply a religious form of atheism. . . . Are they not Gog and Magog? Thus Leontiev had a premonition of the dangers of Pan-Mongolism not only for Russia but also for Europe.

Leontiev's ideas about Russia and her future are of great interest to-day. In his penetrating reflections and presentiments we may find the key to the historical tragedy in which we are participating, and of which he was able to define the character better than any other 'right' or 'left' thinker. But in ideology there was a contradiction which he never resolved. Like many others, he committed the error of thinking that the Revolution in Russia was based exclusively upon the *intelligentsia*, and that it had nothing in common with the people. But at the same time, he discovered in the Russian people an irresistible tendency towards anarchy and extreme movements. Leontiev was mistaken, too, in thinking that the Russian soil was more complex and various than that of contemporary Europe; and that, as a result, Russia would be able to stem the world Socialist and Anarchist revolution. The contrary has proved to be the case, for Russia became the leader of this Revolution, and the passion of the Russian people for equality has exceeded even that of the Western peoples. Even in the nineteenth and twentieth centuries Western Europe was more complex and varied than Russia, and the traditions of its aristocratic culture were still strong. But contradicting himself, Leontiev felt and foresaw that Russia did provide a favourable soil for the Revolution, for the confusion and *levelling* which the Russian people would attempt to impose upon the West. Leontiev did not perceive the religious importance of the problem; nor had he any suspicion of the positive truth which the Russian people would contribute to its solution. The contradiction in Leontiev's philosophical doctrine arose from the divergence between the naturalist and spiritualist points of view. He never succeeded in reconciling them. And this contradiction divided his religious conscience.

CHAPTER VI

THE RELIGIOUS PATH. DUALISM. PESSIM-
ISTIC ATTITUDE ON LIFE. RELIGIOUS
PHILOSOPHY. THE ORTHODOXY OF
FILARET AND KHOMYAKOV. ATTITUDE
TO CATHOLICISM. TRANSCENDENTAL
RELIGION AND MYSTICISM. NATURAL-
ISM AND APOCALYPSE. ATTITUDE TO
ELDERS. ATTITUDE TO DEATH. CON-
CLUSION.

I

It may be asked whether Leontiev had a religious doctrine, a religious lore and a religious philosophy? In the strict sense of the word, he was not as well equipped in these matters as Vladimir Solovyev. He was an anti-gnostic type in his spiritual outlook. Contemplation did not interest him; nor did the nature of God and the Divine mysteries. He was, in fact, no theologian. For lack of training he was out of his depth in theological matters; he was no peer of either Khomyakov or Solovyev in this sphere. Nor had he any consistent religious and philosophical doctrine. In his eyes faith was equivalent to a violation of reason, but he attached the greatest importance to this violation. He was blind to the true reasons that led men to God. As a religious type he was diametrically opposed to the immanent and monistic types; he had a pronounced dualistic and transcendental bias, which was likewise reflected in his aesthetic preoccupation with opposites and contrasts, with the play of light and shade. In his opinion fear was a bilateral form, and love a unilateral one. He therefore gave fear an ascendency over love in his system of religious life. Needless to say, he was thereby led into an error. He had a horror of identity, and insisted upon the validity of the dualistic principle of attraction and repulsion. A sense of divergence was necessary to him before he could summon up any religious feelings. His interest for us lies not so much in his doctrinal contribution as in his religious vocation and destiny. His doctrine was riddled with errors, but it mattered less than the history of his life and the destiny he espoused. His religious destiny was, indeed, an unusual and exceptional one. His life was in itself a remarkable religious fact, a religious phenomenon. It served in itself as a greater religious example than did his writings, although he has ever had many disciples. His religious life served rather to demonstrate that the fundamental problems of life could not be resolved from the standpoint of Christianity, interpreted as the dualistic religion of transcendental egoism.

Leontiev's religion was not a superfluous luxury, a disinterested form of contemplation making for a complex spiritual life, but a matter of life and death, of an exclusively personal salvation and damnation. In this sense he was a medieval man, haunted by a profound fear of eternal damnation. His whole religious experience was a passionate quest of salvation and deliverance from this fear. It assumed for him an essentially religious significance. He came to regard it as an essential part of the Christian religion. Thus, until his dying day religion brought him no peace, tranquillity or radiant joy. He never succeeded in mastering his fear,—his pre-Christian and ancient fear, complicated still further by the terrifying visions of the Medieval Hell. In R. Otto's terminology, it was the *Mysterium Tremendum*. But Leontiev was not satisfied with the experience of this fear, he also made a doctrine of it. 'One must live,' he wrote to Alexandrov, 'one must grow up to a *real* fear of God, an almost animal and elementary fear of the teaching of the Church, an elementary *fear* of sinning.'

Fear was at the foundation of Leontiev's religious attitude, of his spiritual crisis; and it became lastingly associated with his religious aspiration and quest of perfection. 'Animal fear *appears* to debase us. So much the better: let us prostrate ourselves before God; we shall thereby become ethically more perfect. That *love of God, which is so perfect as to banish fear,* is only attainable by the few.' Before he became converted to Orthodoxy, he 'loved *wilfully,* without *law* or fear'. 'But when in 1869, 1870 and 1871, I was stricken by one blow after another, and my health unexpectedly failed, then I suddenly felt helpless in face of the invisible and chastising powers and was frightened into a state of animal fear; *and then only did I feel myself* to be really humiliated and needful of Divine rather than human help.' Leontiev believed that the highest and most serious form of religious experience was founded not on plenitude (love) but on want (fear), not on man's strength but on his weakness. And both his spiritual type and his spiritual life were determined by this fact. He defended Christianity as the religion of fear, not the religion of love. 'Fear is the beginning of wisdom (that is, of real faith), love is but the *fruit.* And the fruit can never be a root.' In describing his conversion Leontiev said: 'I began to have *fear* of God and of the Church. In the course of time the *physical* fear abated but the spiritual fear persisted, and *increased.*' Recalling his former life in the East, he wrote: 'What I lacked then was a *great* sorrow; there was no shadow of *humility*, I had faith *in myself.* I was then far happier than I had been in my youth, and was therefore extremely self-satisfied. But in 1869 came a *sudden* break; one blow followed another. For the first time I *clearly* felt the hand of God above me, and wished to submit to it and rely upon its support against the *most savage* storm raging within me.'

Thus Leontiev's religion was exclusively one of personal salvation, of *transcendental egoism,* as he called it himself with his accustomed boldness and independence of expression. 'To the ringing of monastery bells, recalling ceaselessly the already imminent eternity, he would have liked to become indifferent to everything in the world except his own soul and the work of its purification.' While instructing one young man in quest of the true life, Leontiev questioned his simple servant girl, Varya, in his presence as follows: 'What comes first in the matter of faith: the salvation of self or that of others? Now, I say to her, they are all eager to save others. And Varya, here is another point: how can I set out *to save the souls of others* when I am not sure of saving myself from hell?' 'Yes,' he wrote to Alexandrov, 'preoccupation with the personal salvation of one's soul is transcendental *egoism*; but he who believes in the Evangel and in the Holy Trinity must first of all attend to this. *Altruism* will come in its own good time.' Thus Leontiev's transcendental egoism was born of the fear of eternal damnation and eternal torments, of physical fear, transmuted into spiritual fear. He had no thirst for universal salvation, for the salvation of mankind and the world, which is so characteristic of many Russians. His religious type was diametrically opposed to that of N. Feodorov, who was concerned first of all with the salvation of all, with 'the communal task'. He likewise had nothing in common with, and detested, Dostoievsky's religious views. There was no reference in his writing to the *Sobornost* which was a favourite topic with the Slavophils. He had no sympathy for the ideas of the illumination and transfiguration of the world, of theosis, of the divinization of the creature. His Christianity was anti-cosmic. But he was a strong and traditional adherent of the Church, much more so than either Feodorov, Dostoievsky or the Slavophils. He was heading straight for the monastery and that is where he did end. The authority of the ecclesiastical hierarchy had a permanent significance for him. He tamed his unbridled, restless and pagan nature to obedience. But then he was not converted to Orthodoxy in Russia, but was a religious disciple of Mount Athos and the Greeks. His Orthodoxy was not essentially Russian, but Byzantine in character, monastic and ascetic in outlook, authoritative and hierarchical in structure. Typically Russian religious experiences and aspirations were as a rule more freedom-loving and prophetically inspired. These Leontiev judged to be insufficiently austere and ecclesiastically minded.

Leontiev's religious vocation was a hard and tragic one. There was an ascetic poverty about his religiosity. Whatever richness there was came from the conflict of his religion with his pagan nature. He belonged to an unhappy religious type. On its dark and torturing side, an unhappiness of this sort is a destiny of its own. And ultimately we can never discover why such a destiny should have been the lot of this or that man. It does not imply that God has forsaken such a man, that He does not love him or provide for him. Such a man may come to occupy a higher place in the Kingdom of Heaven than men of a more joyful and radiant religious disposition. But the fact is that in this earthly life Leontiev experienced but few religious ecstasies, blessed communions with God and visions of Divine mysteries. His joys were pagan joys, aesthetic joys, rather than religious ones. But he finally realized that his attempts to live an aesthetic life, and the joys accompanying it, were but an illusion and self-deception. His religious and Christian life, on the other hand, was full of suffering, sorrow and sadness. His Christianity was a gloomy one, but then he could not abide 'pink' Christianity. His dual life persisted to the end: he was a pagan and aesthete in everyday life, and a Christian ascetic in the religious life, his eyes fixed on the world hereafter, his feet set on the path of monasticism. Thus he blended in himself Alcibiades and Golgotha, the Renaissance and monasticism; but these opposites were co-existent rather than organically blended and transmuted. He felt that there was no salvation for him in this world, that the world was too great a temptation for him, and he turned to salvation in the other world, in monasticism.

Leontiev's aestheticism was an obstacle to his leading a Christian life in this world. He was never able to overcome his pagan nature, to renounce the stirring Renaissance spirit in him. Only Mount Athos and the Optina Monastery were able to calm and soothe his worldly passions, to give him the feeling that the joys and ecstasies of worldly beauty were so much vanity and dross. His passion for Islam was not accidental; his whole Christianity was permeated by it. He had a greater consciousness of God the Father than of God the Son: of an awe-inspiring, remote, severe and transcendental

Deity, than of a loving, charitable, familiar and immanent Deity, of God the Redeemer. His attitude to God was governed above all by fear and submission rather than by intimacy and love. He had a strongly developed feeling for the Church but a less strongly developed feeling for the Person of Christ. Indeed, he hardly ever mentioned Christ. The only passages he quoted from the Gospel and the Holy Scriptures were those in which it was said that love and truth would never triumph on earth. The pessimistic notes of the Apocalypse were nearest to his heart. His indignation was excited most of all by attempts to interpret Christianity in a humanitarian way. 'Humanitarian pseudo-Christianity with its senseless all-forgiveness, with its cosmopolitanism, with its absence of a clear dogma, with its sermon of love, but without the injunction of "faith and the fear of God", without any ceremonial—the symbol of an essentially true doctrine, —such a Christianity is, indeed, but the *Revolution*, however much coated over with sugar. Such a Christianity makes war and government impossible; and what reason is there left to worship God. . . . Such a Christianity can only hasten universal destruction. Its very meekness is criminal.'

Rozanov said rightly of Leontiev, that he had the temerity to rebel against 'Christian meekness'. Thus before Nietzsche's time he was that rare phenomenon, a Nietzschean Christian. He was right to protest against the confusion of humanism and Christianity, but the whole problem was more complex than he imagined. He himself confused Dostoievsky's idea of love with Tolstoy's, and treated with suspicion every experience of blessed love in humanism. He made many witty and penetrating attacks on this 'sweetened' Christianity. Monks were men after his own heart because they were all 'pessimists with regard to Europeanism, liberty, equality and man's life on this earth in general. . . . They believe that wars, family quarrels, inequalities, diseases, are not only *inevitable* but also occasionally even *necessary* for men'. '*Truth* lies not in "rights and liberty" but in something quite different, heart-rending for those who seek visible harmony and peace on earth, quite tolerable and even pleasant at times if we look upon life as something stormy and fascinating, partly tedious, partly very agreeable, but in any case an evanescent dream. In the light of this one accepts as a matter of principle obligations and sufferings, men's disappointments and defects; neither weariness in the vain pursuit of personal happiness, nor momentary explosions of rage and anger, can ever become a conceited and constant protest. A pessimistic outlook on *humanity as a whole* and a personal belief in Divine Providence and in our impotence and unwisdom, help to reconcile man not only with his own life but with the *power of others*, and with the revolting eternal tragedy of history.' In these words there is a subtle blend of Christian asceticism and pagan aestheticism, of religious pessimism and joyous experience. . . . 'I do not believe that life could ever become the temple of a complete world and of absolute truth. . . . Such a hope and belief in humanity contradicts the teaching of the Evangel. The Gospel and the Apostles say that *the further we shall go, the worse it will be;* and they counsel us only to preserve intact *our personal faith and our personal virtues to the end.*'

It was characteristic of Leontiev's religious psychology that those pessimistic Christian prophecies should have been a source of joy to him, that he should have been almost in raptures at the thought that truth would not triumph on earth and that bliss was impossible. He did not aspire to realize truth or perfection on earth. And in this his pessimism coincided with his aesthetic need for polarity, and the contrast of light and shade. 'On the one hand, sorrow, ills, stormy passions, crime, envy, persecutions, mistakes; and on the other, unexpected consolations, kindness, forgiveness, simplicity and a joyful heart! That is the only possible *life* on this earth, the only possible *harmony* under these stars. *The harmonious law of compensation, and that is all*. The poetic living concordance of bright and dark colours, *and that is all*.' The triumph of the bright colours alone would not have satisfied his aesthetic taste. It might even be maintained, that the existence of evil was for him both a religious and an aesthetic necessity. There was almost a malevolence in his exclamation: 'And towards the end, not only will *universal fraternity not* be realized, but *love will become poorer when the Gospel will be preached in all the corners of the world*. And when this prophecy will reach the point of satiation prescribed to it from above, when with the impoverishment of even that love, however incomplete and palliative, men will begin to believe madly in "peace and tranquillity", then it will be that perdition will encompass them . . . and they will not escape it!'

We have seen that Leontiev was personally a kindly enough man. But there was an element of wrath in his penetrating antinomian speculation that helped him to discover much that was concealed from well-intentioned and philanthropic thinkers. 'Both the poetry of earthly life and the conditions of salvation hereafter necessitate neither a sort of *continuous* and impossible love, nor a constant animosity, but speaking objectively, a sort of *harmonious tension of hostility*

[200]

and love, in face of higher ends.' Here we have the same insistence on contrasts, polarities, contradictions, and the same
dislike of monism in the religious life. Positive science and
positive religion become reconciled in the impossibility of
truth and prosperity on earth. Love will remain forever
merely the antidote of evil, rather than become the very air
breathed by men. Real truth must accept 'that gloomy and
austere pessimism, that virile humility which, believing in
the incorrigibility of earthly life, says: Have patience! *Things
will never be better for all.* It will be better for some, worse for
others. This state of fluctuating sorrow and pain is the only
possible *harmony* on earth! And do not expect *anything else*.
. . . *There is nothing true in the real phenomenal world.* There is
only *one* true, exact and indubitable fact, and *that is,* that
everything here must perish! And so why all this feverish
anxiety about the earthly happiness of future generations?
Why all these infantile sickly dreams and enthusiasms? Our
day is our age! And therefore be *patient* and attend either to
practical immediate needs or in matters of affection to the
people who are nearest you. *Yes, attend to the people nearest
you rather than to the whole of mankind*'.

There is a religious, ethical and aesthetic truth in the
phrase, 'Everything here must perish.' An awareness of this
truth is spiritually invigorating. The Christian consciousness
that all earthly things are instable and transitory, that eternity
will be realized only after the destruction of the earth and of
all living creatures upon it, liberates and cures us of the harmful and perverse utopias of earthly paradise. The prophecy of
the reign of Christ upon earth is not a Christian and Orthodox one, but rather a universal humanitarian one. 'All the
positive religions which, through their direct or indirect

[201]

influence, gave birth to the principal cultures of this planet, were *pessimistic* in their teaching, and they *legalized* the suffering, the wrongs, and the untruth of this life. . . . All Christian thinkers were also pessimists in their way. They even concluded that evil, wrongs and sorrow were highly *necessary* and even indispensable to us.' Not only the Christian but every other religion must admit that man's burden of suffering has a purpose transcending the limits of this life; they must reconcile themselves to life with its trials, horrors and misfortunes. Revolt and rebellion are not in their nature religious. 'From the Christian standpoint it can be said, that *the reign of perpetual* peace, prosperity, concord and general security,—all that democratic progress has so unsuccessfully espoused,—would be the greatest imaginable calamity in the Christian sense. . . . The philosophical idea of complex development towards an *unknown* goal can be reconciled to Christianity; but the eudaemonic idea of a progress founded upon the quest of happiness through liberty and equality, is completely incompatible with the fundamental idea of Christianity.' Christ said that mankind was *incorrigible* in a general sense; He also said that, before the end, love would grow poorer. In Leontiev's opinion self-willed love is so 'practical' that it leads to revolution. 'A willing humility before the Lord is a better and *surer means of saving the soul* than this proud and untenable defence of paternal mildness and ever-ready *unction*. Many of the Saints preferred life in the desert to *active* love; there they *prayed to God first of all* for their own soul, and *then* for that of others. . . . Even in monastic communities the experienced Elders do not encourage too great a passion for active and burning love, but in the first place teach *obedience, compulsion and the passive forgiveness of wrongs.*' Most of these trenchant thoughts were to be found in Leontiev's article, *Our New Christians,* in which he attacked both Tolstoy and Dostoievsky for being 'pink' or philanthropic Christians. Leontiev had an irreconcilable hatred for this species of Christianity. But he failed to distinguish sufficiently between Tolstoy and Dostoievsky; and he also failed to grasp that the latter's Christianity was tragic in character. He was also blind not only to the fact that humanism was nearer to Christianity than bestialism, but that it was also Christian in its origin.

'Christian asceticism presupposes struggle, suffering and inequality; it remains true to the *phenomenal* philosophy of strict realism. The eudaemonic faith, on the other hand, aspires to do away with *pain*, that essential attribute of every historical as well as animal *phenomenology*. . . . In practice Christianity is more consistent with the earthly life than are these frigid hopes of omni-utilitarian progress!' This was a recurrent theme with Leontiev. In his eyes Christianity was both more ideal and more real than the eudaemonic doctrine of progress and happiness on earth. He claimed that it was his mental pride that made him so humble towards the Church. 'I do not believe that my mind is infallible; nor do I believe in the infallibility of other minds, even the greatest; and still less do I believe in the infallibility of collective mankind; but in order to live, everyone must believe in something. I shall believe in the Gospel as expounded by the Church, but not otherwise. O Lord, what a boon, what a relief! How lucid everything is! And yet no pursuit is thwarted, whether it be aesthetics, patriotism, philosophy, science rightly comprehended, proper love of mankind.'

Ascetic and monastic Christianity was not only strict and

austere, it was also indulgent to human weaknesses and failings, as Leontiev learnt from his intercourse with the Elders. The Elders were indulgent to the personality, but merciless to the temptations and illusions of earthly progress and prosperity. Rozanov once said, that when Leontiev happened to meet a liberal, he became a 'black' monk with big staff and used it to thump the liberal on the head. When it was a question of man's earthly happiness, human illusions, Liberalism, Democracy, Socialism or Anarchism, Leontiev became an austere ascetic. But he had another side to his nature, sympathetic to individual people and individual souls, the flowering of cultures, and the great historic values. He was indulgent to human weaknesses and sins, human defects and failings, but had no mercy for false beliefs and principles however exalted. 'Evil passions are better in monks than lofty but unsuitable and improper principles.' 'For the Orthodox principle, the seed of harm and destruction does not lie in the personal delicts of Christians, nor yet in their crude material motives, grasping quarrels, crimes even, but rather in *its gradual transmutation* into other principles.' '*It is even essential for the higher ends of monkhood* that the majority of monks should be imperfect and sinful. If all monks were like angels in fact as well as in aspiration or in ideal, then the monasteries would be unable to produce their Saints, their great ascetics and their Elders. From the Christian point of view, it is incomparably more permissible for us to indulge our weakness for enjoyment occasionally than to preach the heresy of a godless ethics and an improbable universal love.'

Leontiev had an antipathy to moralistic religion; and he was particularly hostile to any substitution of moral and humanistic principles for religious ones. According to him

[204]

Christianity did not admit the autonomous morality of the human personality. He had a deep-rooted dislike of 'Evangelical' Christianity, of any interpretation of Christ independent of the Church, of the transfer of the centre of gravity of the religious life to the Gospel Commandments. He had grasped the fact that for Christianity the institution of the Church was synonymous with the principle of development. 'To be an Orthodox Christian, *it is essential to read the Gospel in the light of the teaching of the Holy Fathers;* otherwise the Scriptures can justify any number of false doctrines such as Lutherism, Skoptism (sect of the castrated), and others.' The history of the Church requires the co-operation not only of the pure-minded and the clean-hearted, but also of the cruel and the cunning. From the Orthodox point of view depraved and immoral men may be of greater service than the virtuous ones. . . . 'Charity, Goodness, Justice, Self-Denial, all these qualities can only manifest themselves when there is sorrow, inequality, wrong, and cruelty.' 'An arbitrary *morality* such as practised by honest atheists has *not the slightest* value for the purposes of salvation hereafter.'

'When a spiritual or mystical feeling dominates a passionate aestheticism, I respect it, I bow to it, I revere and adore it. But when a utilitarian ethics dominates this mysterious poetry, so indispensable to the plenitude of vital development, I am indignant; and I have little hope of that society which this can happen too often!' 'Charity, Goodness Forgiveness. . . . They have borrowed but one aspect Gospel teaching and they call it *the essential aspect!* they forgotten asceticism and austerity? Have the linger over the severe and wrathful words of th One cannot take only the tender, sweet, ple forting elements, and leave out the stern, severe and torturing ones.' Thus Leontiev looked upon Byzantinism as the true development of Christianity. 'There never was, nor is, nor ever will be any truth on earth. Nor should there ever be. In the presence of human truth men would forget the Divine truth!'

Leontiev established a distinction between 'charitable' or moral love on the one hand, and 'rapturous' or aesthetic love on the other. All his instincts made him inclined towards the latter. That was his worldly definition of love. In the religious sphere he treated with suspicion any form of love that savoured of autonomous morality and humanism, and that dispensed with fear. Such love was 'the wilful product of *anthropolatry*, the new belief in *an earthly man* and in an earthly humanity.' 'We are *all* living and breathing daily in *human fear*, in fear of a greedy reckoning, of egoism, of poverty, of some secret humiliation; in fear of punishment, of want, of disease, of wrong; and yet we think that this is "all right", and that our dignity is not affected. But then, is the loftier fear, the fear of sin, a vulgar, common fear? Is the fear of straying from or not growing up to the doctrine of the Church a cowardly fear, a woman's fear?' Leontiev carried his antipathy to moralism and rationalism to such lengths that he would have sooner tolerated sects like the Mormons, the *Chlysty* and the *Scopts,* than his contemporaries of the Protestant persuasion. Thus Leontiev was a convinced Orthodox Christian within the limits of a particular Orthodox tradition, but he was never completely a Christian in the wider sense. He never emerged from the framework of the legalistic, Old Testament religiosity. And as a result, his outlook was not entirely Christian.

II

Leontiev disapproved of that Slavonic and Democratic trend in the Orthodox Church which was in favour of a rapprochement with Anglicanism. 'The new Slavonic-Anglican Orthodoxy is a more dangerous (and perhaps more fruitless) manifestation than any sect like the *Scopts* or the *Chlysty*. . . . These latter have at least a heretical creativeness about them, a Satanic poetry of their own, a *structure*, a plasticity, that *distinguishes* them at once *as a group* from Orthodoxy. But what promise does this Anglo-Slavonic bourgeois clergy hold out except sinfulness and spiritual rebellion, on the one hand, and stupidity and prose, on the other? For whom and why is it necessary for some Madame Blagoviestchenskaya or Madame Usspenskaya to sit by her husband on the steps of the episcopal throne?' Leontiev had doubts about the authenticity of Khomyakov's Orthodoxy, discerning a Protestant and humanistic tendency in him. *Filaret* was for him the authentic type of Orthodox thinker: his catechism was more true than that of Khomyakov. Leontiev failed to perceive that, in his Church doctrine, the Metropolitan Filaret was less Orthodox and more Protestant than Khomyakov. But Leontiev used the term 'Filaret' in a specific symbolical sense. He disliked free 'literary' excursions into the sphere of ecclesiastical and theological problems. 'I was taught to believe in and serve Byzantine Orthodoxy ┃ Hieronymus and Makary, the famous confessors of M┃ Athos. This Byzantine Orthodoxy (and not Khomya┃ has still its adherents among such preachers as Ni┃ Odessa and Ambrose of Kharkov; and in fact, am┃ famous representatives of contemporary Rus┃

ticism and of the Russian ecclesiastical hierarchy. In Leon-tiev's eyes, this Byzantine Orthodoxy was one and the same as Filaret's. 'A man may be *personally* a good, pious and vir-tuous Christian, within the framework of both Filaret's and Khomyakov's type of Orthodoxy; and there have been and still are such men. But there is a greater certainty of becom-ing a Saint under the older persuasion, that of Filaret, than under the new Slavophil one.' This contention of Leontiev's was disproved by the example of Saint Seraphim, who was neither a Byzantine nor a Filaret type.

The Slavophil idea of the *Sobornost* did not attract Leon-tiev because he thought that he discerned in it certain popular and democratic tendencies. He was a decided supporter of the hierarchical principle in the Church, a Catholic rather than Orthodox trait in him. He regarded monasticism as the very flower of the Orthodox religion. By way of contrast, Slavophil Orthodoxy was popular and social rather than monastic in its appeal. Christianity, as Leontiev saw it, was 'founded upon an untiring submission to Christ'. The Slavo-phils, on the other hand, interpreted it primarily as the free-dom of the spirit. But Leontiev had a different conception of Byzantine Orthodoxy: 'In the sphere of political, society and family life, it is a religion of *discipline*. In the sphere of our inner emotional life, it is a religion of *disillusionment,* a reli-gion without hope for any earthly thing.' This contrasted with the Russian domestic and social character and with the earthly aspirations of Slavophil Orthodoxy. Khomyakov's doctrine was a very benign one compared with Leontiev's. 'It may be possible to found a Slavonic Church. But would it be a true Orthodox Church? Would the State illuminated by this Church prove strong and enduring? It may be possible to break away from the Greek Churches and forget their great traditions; we may pause and consider Khomyakov's idea that the Church cannot survive without a hierarchy but can live without monasticism; and having espoused this false idea with liberal affection, it would not be difficult to dissolve the monasteries one by one, and to admit married bishops. Thereafter the transition would be easy to that future *Russian* Orthodoxy, as outlined by Hilyarev-Platonov, and which I have already described as 'a return to pre-Constantinian times, that is, as an abandonment of even the Nicaean symbol of faith, without the compensation of those stimulating persecutions launched by the Pagan Emperors'.

But Leontiev did not foresee that the actual return of the Orthodox Church to pre-Constantinian times was, perhaps, the beginning of a new and creative period in Christianity. 'For all my sincere respect for the older Slavophil teachers, Khomyakov, Samarin, and Aksakov, I must confess that their sincere labours often *instil* doubts in me ... and in the light of *further* rash conclusions, fear even. Orthodoxy is capable of further *development,* but certainly not in the direction of a sort of *national Protestantism;* much sooner in the opposite direction, towards unity with Rome, or better still *it might learn* a great deal from Rome as one learns from an opponent, adapting only her *strong points, without any identity of interest.*' Leontiev felt that he had on the whole a greater affinity with Solovyev than with Khomyakov. 'Solovyev's thought is incomparably clearer and more tangible than Khomyakov's (with Khomyakov "love" is but love, "truth" is but truth, and no more); I confess to not understanding *anything* of his theology, and I am still convinced that *Filaret's* older doctrine is both more comprehensible and *authentic.*' In the same way, he esteemed Pobiedonostzev higher than Dostoievsky in ecclesiastical matters. Nevertheless, we are obliged to admit that Khomyakov was more representative of Russian Orthodoxy than Leontiev, who tended to stylize rather than to express the Orthodox faith. And there is something alarming in the fact, that the Elders of Optina approved more of Leontiev than of the Slavophils, Gogol, Dostoievsky, and Vladimir Solovyev, that they accepted his spiritual temper as being truly Orthodox.

III

Leontiev not only did not share the Slavophils' traditional antipathy to Catholicism, but he had definite Catholic sympathies. These grew stronger towards the end of his life. In this connection, his relations with Vladimir Solovyev were of some importance. 'On reading him, a hope is born anew, that the Orthodox Church has an *earthly* future as well as a heavenly one. . . . The fact that Solovyev was the first to rouse a whole storm of religious ideas on the sleepy surface of our ecclesiastical sea is in itself no mean service! This is no rationalism, no belief after the manner of Pashkovsky or the Stundists, no slow trickle into the abyss of unbelief, but on the contrary a movement against the older current, against our accustomed semi-Protestant trend; it even "goes against our grain".' Solovyev proved to be a great stimulus to Leontiev, and excited in him 'tempests of religious thoughts'. But Leontiev was timid and meek in comparison to Solovyev; he did not presume to figure as a religious innovator. 'If I were categorically told from *on high*, by the hierarchy, that there is *no salvation for me outside of the Roman Church,* and that I had to renounce my Russian nationality for the sake of this salvation, I should not hesitate to renounce it. . . . But I have not yet been commanded to do so by the All-Eastern Council, the Eastern Patriarchs or the Holy Russian Synod! In my eyes Solovyev has neither personal mystical unction nor the collective power of a spiritual Council. . . . The most terse, dry and ill-arranged catechism has a million times more weight for me, as an Orthodox Christian, than all Solovyev's learning and talent! . . . I shall follow Solovyev's lead without fear, for about half-way; but can his genius prevent my Orthodox reason from taking leave of him at the crossroads, and, while acknowledging my indebtedness to him, from saying at the last moment: "The *fear of sin* does not allow me to accompany you further. The Bishops and the Elders have not done so, nor shall I. . . ." I *love* your ideas and feelings; I am ready to admire your mind with all the sincerity of my unenvious nature, but I shall not only not follow in your steps myself, I shall speak frankly to anyone, who asks my opinion, thus: "Read and admire him; follow him within *certain limits* towards the peak of his *spiritual pyramid;* but in the depths of your heart beware of sinning against the Church in which you were baptied and reared." '

The gulf between Solovyev and Leontiev is here made apparent. Solovyev felt inspired to a prophetic vocation within the Church; he presumed to be a creator in the religious sphere, to probe the sacred and Divine mysteries. Leontiev, on the other hand, was primarily concerned with his own salvation in the Church; he showed himself humble and obedient; he sought refuge in the Church from his sinful worldly excesses. He asked the help of the Elders to liberate him from his demoniac will. Thus, while Leontiev

[211]

was a type of the worldly Renaissance, Solovyev was a type of the spiritual and religious Renaissance. Therefore the free and daring exercise of their minds was confined to different spheres. Leontiev showed no interest in theosophical and theocratic investigations. He did not feel he had the prophetic vocation in him; he was afraid of religious innovation as a hindrance and menace to his personal salvation. He advised Dostoievsky, for example, to study rather than to preach. But he had a greater confidence in Solovyev, and learned what he could from him. In arguing with him he was always timid, humble and not too sure of himself. There was the same diffidence in his discussion with Solovyev about the Papacy and the union of the Churches. His decided personal prejudices were an obstacle in these arguments. He liked the Catholics for their religious fanaticism, for their strong and active faith; he thought that the Catholics 'might serve us as a good example'. In his opinion 'Catholics are very useful not only for Europe but *also for Russia*'. He sympathized with the idea of a union of the Churches, and believed that Solovyev's advocacy of this measure was serving a useful purpose. 'It is useful for two reasons: in the first place, because of its *Pan-Christian* mysticism; and in the second, because of that *necessity of lucid spiritual discipline* which is manifest in all its loftiest labours.'

To counteract extreme Nihilism other extremes were necessary,—those of religion and mysticism rather than bourgeois ethics. In Leontiev's opinion, Catholicism had a tremendous power of resistance to Nihilism and revolutionary depredation, a greater power than Orthodoxy. 'When it is a question of *development, originality, cultural and religious creativeness, I cannot help perceiving* that, after the schism of the Churches, Byzantine Christianity ceased to develop, and that Russia (and the Slavs in general) adopted it *without any modifications* or, in other words, without *creativeness*. But it was only after the Schism, that European culture as such began to assume its peculiar and non-Byzantine character. The history of Catholicism is marked by constant *creativeness*, originality, independence and strength.'

These just observations must have profoundly shocked the Slavophils and our Church nationalists. 'We are all (and I more than others!) impotent,' he wrote to Alexandrov. 'The Orthodox faith has no really good champions. . . . Is there no hope at all of a lasting and profound renascence of Truth and Faith in this unfortunate (and abject!) Russia of ours? . . . For many and weighty reasons I cannot refute this. My "strings" have evidently become frayed from over-patience, and for lack of *timely* support. . . . I would take wing, but I can not. The spirit has left me.' He wrote this after his break with Solovyev, when he decided to oppose him. But could he very well challenge Solovyev, in view of his attitude to ecclesiastical and national questions?

Leontiev retained his freedom of thought and opinion on theological questions, although he had surrendered his life to the keeping of the Elders. He did not think it possible to limit the life of the Church by concentrating only on the preservation of the known, the experienced and the generally accepted. 'Laymen can and should think and write about *new* problems.' The hallmark of a Christian was simplicity of heart rather than simplicity of mind. 'What an insignificant thing this "religion" would be, if it could not support an educated and developed mind!' But Leontiev himself was unable to profit by the desired freedom of religious and theological speculation. The fear of damnation and the thirst for salvation clipped his wings and undermined his creative originality. 'A Higher Will informs me that it is better for the salvation of my soul to keep silence and be humble.'

Towards the end of his life his writing lost some of its vividness, penetration and daring. To his dying day he failed to attain a 'simplicity of mind'. 'I have worldly ties, I have the bad habit of writing, I have the great misfortune to be a Russian literary man.' In a letter he wrote to Father Foudel, Leontiev returned to the theme of a 'simple or complex mind'. On this occasion he argued in favour of a 'complex' mind. He also frequently referred to the question that troubled him so much,—his break with Solovyev. In his opinion, Solovyev's idea of the development of the Church' was the one that would survive; but the repercussions of his thought would be great. 'I shall not conceal from you my "infirmity",' he wrote to Father Foudel. 'The idea of Papal Infallibility appeals to me *very much indeed*. "The Elder of Elders." If I were in Rome I should not hesitate twice to kiss Leo XIII's toe, much less his hand. . . . Roman Catholicism appeals equally to my sincerely despotic tastes, my propensity to obedience, and my mind and heart for many other reasons.'

Leontiev's relations with Father Clement Zederholm, and their discussions, are a matter of great interest. Father Zederholm was not by nature an Elder or a spiritual guide. Leontiev was fond of discussions with him, of revealing to him the whole complexity of his nature and his mind. Their intercourse was worldly and cultural as well as spiritual. Leontiev would have liked to see in Church circles 'more people like Clement, endowed with worldly education and learning, but submitting by an act of will and by conviction to the severe imperatives of the Church dogma.' In his talks with Father Clement Leontiev often showed himself a Renaissance character, an ancient pagan and aesthete, an infinitely complex and contradictory personality. Father Clement would tell him that the Devil was taking advantage of his aesthetic proclivities and his love of the poetic life. He wished to control Leontiev's imagination and to instil in him the fear of even the most innocent sympathy for heresy. But Leontiev would not abjure either his complex imagination or his aesthetic interests. The spiritual crisis of 1871 had not finally transformed him or made him renounce his love of polarity, complexity, earthly beauty and nature. Father Clement insisted that he should 'feel a spiritual loathing for everything that was not Orthodox'. But Leontiev retorted, 'Why should I feel such a loathing? No! I find that impossible. . . . I take pleasure in reading the Koran. . . .'—'The Koran!' exclaimed Father Clement, turning away. 'What an abomination!'—'But in my eyes it is a beautiful lyrical poem,' replied Leontiev. 'I shall never agree with your point of view. I cannot understand such one-sidedness, and you are only thinking of my welfare. . . . I have a greater esteem for the Jesuit than for an indifferent priest, who does not care whether the grass stops growing and who will not cross himself unless it thunders.' On another occasion Leontiev really frightened Father Clement by saying: 'As you see, I am at the mercy of everything: my mind will not admit of simplification. I give it free rein with ideas; this might be a waste of time, but my fundamental faith is in no way shaken. Let us take an example. I have at home a copy of Voltaire's

Dictionnaire Philosophique. I once read in it the article about the Prophet David. Voltaire proved that in his own day he would have been fit only for the galleys . . . and other things of that kind. . . . And I was very amused. . . . *I like the power of the intelligence, but I do not believe in the infallibility of reason. . . . And I find that one thing does not exclude another.* Half-an-hour after reading Voltaire, I could pray as before quite sincerely in the words of the Psalms of David. . . . I do cross myself and go to Church, and try to fulfil my religious duties like any of those old women who gather outside your hermitage gates. Therefore, let me not disguise my fears for the whole of Christianity and the whole world, when I see how deeply Catholicism, the mightiest and most expressive of the bases of the social edifice, is shaken. Let me be free to regret all those variegated monks, in hoods and broad-brimmed hats, the pomp of processions, the red-robed cardinals. The highest manifestations of poetry and politics are more deeply related than is generally believed. When poetry declines, so does political power, and even profound thought. Was it not you who were envying not so long ago the greater depth and expressiveness of the Western peoples? *But all cracks have depth.'*

This passage from Leontiev is more than usually characteristic. Only an aristocrat, a *barin*, could speak in this way. The democratic bias of religiosity does not admit of this intellectual juggling, this love of contrasts, this freedom, this juxtaposition of the psalms of David and Voltaire. This aristocratic trait was also strongly reflected in his religious experiences. 'What a bore! Why should I be forced to be a brother of some German or French democrat, whose illustrated portrait even is a source of irritation to me? As a

Christian I am compelled to suppress this *artistic* squeamishness of mine. . . . But if I am *not* a Christian? Then only fear, when confronted with this mob of undeveloped men, can keep me silent.' Thus brotherhood in Christ did not, mean for Leontiev a fraternity of equals. In his opinion, too, the nobility were more creatively gifted than the clerics. 'I cannot help regretting the uncouth feelings and manners of many of our clergy.' He expressed the hope that more noblemen should take up the monastic life and introduce into the monasteries 'their good breeding, their refined and tempered feelings, their elegance, and their *worldly* poetry'. 'In heaven there neither is, nor will be, an equality of rewards and punishments; and on earth, universal equality and liberty are but the preparation for the reign of Antichrist.'

The demoniac and aesthetic principle retained its value for Leontiev until his death. His love of contrasts was so great that he wrote from Mount Athos: 'Side by side on my table lie Proudhon and the Prophet David, Byron and Chrysostom, John of Damas and Goethe, Khomyakov and Hertzen. Here I am more at peace with myself than in the world; here I still love the world like a distant and harmless picture.' He wanted life to be 'magnificent, rich and varied in its clash of divine (religious) forces and passionate aesthetic or demoniac forces. He was against the complete elimination of Satanic forces, for they were necessary to make life more *varied*. At first he was in favour of variety at all costs, but after his conversion he tended towards a *unity* which should yet not exclude variety. 'Both the Christian doctrine and European "progress",' he wrote to Rozanov, 'are combining to destroy the beauty of life on earth, to destroy life itself. What can we do? We must help the Christian cause even at the expense of our beloved beauty.' There is a sense of anguish in these words, an echo of Nietzsche and Rozanov. But Leontiev never did give up his worship of beauty, his dualism, his contradictory principles. He made Father Clement apprehensive most of all by the sympathy he showed for Catholicism, by his passionate interest in 'cultural and political' Catholicism. At first he failed to understand why Father Clement was so put out by this, but finally he did understand. 'The difference between us was very great. I can never forget that world-wide gigantic cultural struggle which is being waged between a clearly wrought antiquity and a nebulous modernity; but he would not leave alone for a single moment the task of salvation, the salvation not only of his own soul but also that of others. When arguing in favour of certain aspects of the Papacy, I was thinking of the *destiny of Europe and its unfortunately potent influence upon Russia;* but he was anxious and insistent in his objections, thinking *of my soul.* He was alarmed even at this spark of sympathy with the Papacy.'

This incident was characteristic not only of Leontiev, but also of the mood of the Optina Elders and of our Orthodox monasticism in general. Leontiev's religiosity was, indeed, of this kind, but he had also another side to his nature. He was not indifferent to historical destiny. He would have liked the Russian clergy and monks to be less passive and less preoccupied with the salvation of individual souls, and more patterned on the Catholic model. But unlike Vladimir Solovyev, he could never succeed in adapting his Christian beliefs to the interpretation of history. He was not attracted to Catholicism for the same reasons as Solovyev, but because he admired its aesthetic aspects and its political power.

[218]

IV

Deeply disturbed at the time of his religious crisis by the fear of eternal damnation and the active passionate urge for personal salvation, Leontiev was compelled to turn to the Elders for spiritual guidance. Spiritually he was unable to find deliverance within himself. He was not one of those blessed humans who discover the Christ in themselves, who live in a state of profound contemplation of the Divine mysteries, and who know the joy of direct communion with the Deity. Leontiev, on the other hand, was seeking deliverance from his own demoniac nature, a salvation outside himself, a liberation from himself and from his self-destroying will. After his conversion, he wished at once to surrender his soul to the keeping of the Elders and he went to Mount Athos for that purpose. The Elders Makary and Hieronymus were then in residence there. But the moment had not yet come for him to abandon the world. Spiritual peace did not come to him until he retired to the Optina Monastery and met the Elder Ambrose. But after Father Ambrose had become his spiritual guide he did finally reach his haven of peace. In a letter written from Mount Athos, he said: 'Have you any idea what a delight it is to surrender all one's knowledge, education, self-love and pride, to the keeping of some simple, experienced and honest Elder? Do you know how much *Christian will* is needed in order to kill within one that *other worldly will?*'

In his book, *Father Clement Zederholm,* he spoke as follows about the necessity for Elders: 'The remission of sins in confession is not enough for me; I do not always and entirely trust for any length of time Christian humility and the evidence of my conscience, for this latter is founded primarily upon the pride of personal reason. Hence in those difficult moments of my life, when I am persistently assailed by sin and sorrow, I wish to have trust in an impartial man, in a man who understands perfectly but is, if possible, removed from the worries of our world. I do not believe that such a spiritual guide or Elder is sinless or incapable of intellectual sin. No! I come to him with a warm faith in God and in the Church, and of course with personal trust, because of his good life; I come to him, and I shall obediently accept and try to fulfil whatever he may say in reply to my secret confession and even my expressed intentions. And with all that, I, a lay believer, may be personally very clever and highly cultured, and also far more experienced in worldly affairs than this Elder.' Leontiev carried the surrender of his will so far, that he once said to Astafiev's wife, 'Do you know the extent of my obedience to the Elder? Now, were he to command me to kill you, I should do so without a moment's hesitation.' In another letter, written to Gubastov, he spoke of the attitude adopted by the Optina Elders to his literary work: 'They are well disposed towards me and, having acquainted themselves both with my character and my circumstances, they have decided that I should go on with my writing.' Hence Leontiev's literary life proved quite fruitful during his stay in the Optina Monastery. The Elders combined severity with great indulgence, a fact well known to those who have had dealings with them. Father Ambrose's guidance affected not only Leontiev's spiritual life but his material life also. Thus, when Leontiev was offered a post with an important newspaper in Petersburg, Father Ambrose 'did not give his blessing to a refusal, but bid me ask for a

[220]

better salary and conditions'. That was characteristic of the Elders. And Leontiev who knew them well, and had absorbed the spirit of Optina, definitely affirmed that the character of the Elder Zossima had nothing in common with that of the real Elders. 'When Dostoievsky published, in *The Brothers Karamazov*, his hopes of *a triumphant Christianity on earth*, then the archpriests of Optina *laughingly* asked each other, "Is it you, perhaps, Father, who think that?" The *religious censorship* forbade a special edition of *The Doctrine of Father Zossima*, and so did ours, for it was feared that it might give rise to a new heresy.' But the prophetic image of the Elder Zossima was superior to that of the real Elders.

Leontiev did not believe in *the new ways*. 'How can there be any new ways? I have none but those of dogmatic and ascetic Orthodoxy, *which have resisted science and progress*.' He had learnt the lesson from the Elders. But nevertheless he was anxious about the fate of the Optina Monastery, and he felt that the majority of the monks there were too divorced from life. 'The Optina of our time requires a cultured Father Superior, and there is none such among the archpriests there. There are among them active, kindly, and clever practical men; but with the exception of the head monk, Father Anatole, they are all *tradesmen* by birth and outlook. And mark you, they would not elect Father Anatole. They will not elect him because he is too *ideal;* and though they are all honest and sincere monks in their own special sphere, these Elders are much too preoccupied with household duties and give little thought to the historical significance of the Optina Monastery in nineteenth-century Russia and to the importance of its existence to laymen. They are still not very enlightened as to what is happening in the world outside and live in their minds according to "ancient simplicity".' Leontiev's was an immeasurably more complex nature than that of the Optina monks, and his only connection with them was through Father Ambrose. The monks made no attempt to resolve or even pose the disturbing problem of the relation of the ways of salvation and those of creativeness. Nor was that problem capable of solution within the limits of Leontiev's type of Orthodoxy, even though his entire life was tortured by that problem.

Leontiev had no theocratic idea, no desire to find the Kingdom of God. The religious theme of his life lay elsewhere. His love of beauty bound him to the earth and alienated him from the triumph of Christian truth on earth. There was an inner contradiction in his attitude to the future: he believed that happiness could not triumph on earth, because the victory of evil had been foretold; and even if that happiness were realizable, it would itself prove to be the supreme evil. He not only did not believe in the possibility of a Christian community, of a reign of truth and happiness, but he also had no wish to see its realization. He associated such a Christian community with humanist, liberal, equalitarian and progressive tendencies. He refused to see anything Apocalyptic about Dostoievsky's prophecies. He even finally rejected his beloved Solovyev, when he discovered in him the confusion of Christian and progressive humanist principles. The coming of the Kingdom of God did not figure in many of his prayers: he was more alarmed at the possible elimination of contrast, variety and polarity from the world. Shortly before his death, certain apocalyptic elements manifested themselves in his work, but they were of another character. His belief in earthly progress had crumbled long before Solovyev's. 'The New Testament does, indeed, recommend fraternity *as far as possible* and humanity *for the salvation of our individual souls hereafter;* but *nowhere* is it stated in the Holy Scripture that *by means of this humanity men will attain to peace and happiness. Christ did not hold out this promise.*' He had experienced the 'nostalgia of the world', but he was indignant at the way it was exploited to excite 'civil dissatisfaction'. And he suspected that this was the motive behind the aspiration for a 'Christian Community'.

V

The coming end of the world and the advent of Antichrist were presentiments related to Leontiev's attitude to liberal and equalitarian progress. By becoming universal, the process of simplified confusion marked the end, the agony of the world. The anti-Christian spirit was manifest in the later products of humanism,—in Democracy, Socialism and Anarchism. Leontiev had a premonition of a world revolution which would engulf all the sacred beliefs and values of the noble ancient world. In his mind, this revolution was connected with the agency of the anti-Christian spirit. 'There can only be one *final* statement: *an end to everything upon earth! A cessation of history and life.*' In a letter to Alexandrov he wrote, 'Judging by the symptoms our last days are numbered.' In another letter to Gubastov he said, 'In any case the reign of Antichrist draws near, and in the spiritual sense the elect will dwindle.' He sometimes entertained the hope that, after mankind had experienced 'the bitterness of Socialism', it would embark upon a profound religious and spiritual reaction, and that there would be manifest in science itself 'a consciousness of its effective impotence, a courageous penitence and humility before the might and right of an emotional mysticism and faith'. But this hope was not very strong: it lingered for a while and then finally disappeared.

Leontiev's Apocalyptic visions and presentiments of the end differed from those of Dostoievsky and Solovyev; they were more despairing and lacking in chiliastic expectations. But their real peculiarity was that Leontiev *naturalized* the end of the world. The impending doom of mankind assumed in his eyes the appearance of an irrevocable natural death. He diagnosed this approaching end as a biologist, and sensed it as an aesthete. He then religiously sanctified his diagnosis and sensation, adapting it to Christian prophecy. But his Apocalyptical consciousness preserved the biological imprint. He never penetrated into the realm of mystical eschatology, he never found a mystical expression for his presentiments and prefigurations. But he was acutely aware of the anti-Christian nature of revolutionary humanism with its destructive thirst for equality. 'To *arrest* the march of peoples along the path of anti-Christian progress, to postpone the advent of the Antichrist (of that mighty man who will take upon himself to direct all the anti-Christian and anti-Church movements), *it is essential to keep Tsarist power strong and alive.*' But as it happened, Tsarism turned out to be a poor preservative. *Creative* means of preservation were necessary, but Leontiev could not invent them. Reactionary measures could not hope to stem the anti-Christian tide, only religious and social creativeness could be effective. Leontiev's hopes were centred exclusively on 'freezing' as a means of stopping the rot. Leontiev was not exempt from diabolical temptations himself, but they had their roots in the past rather than in the anti-Christian future.

Leontiev was tormented not only by a presentiment of universal death but also by a premonition of his own death. This became particularly acute at the beginning of the 1890's. He took his secret monastic vows partly because he felt the approach of death, and also partly in order to effect an important change in his own life, and thus justify his presentiment of such an event in his life. 'If death be not near,' he wrote to Alexandrov, 'then some new, *grave and important* change is imminent in my life. The symptoms of *the beginning of the end* have already manifested themselves one after another.' He was capable of great vital resistance to death. According to Varya's account, when he was on his deathbed, feverish, half-conscious and half-delirious, he kept repeating: 'We'll still fight on!' or 'No, I must submit', and then again, 'We'll still fight on!' Though a monk and ascetic, Leontiev had a passion for life and its gorgeous flowering. It was difficult for him to reconcile himself to death. The infinitely sad words in which he described his impressions of Father Clement Zederholm's grave, those words on which he ends his book about him, convey his mental struggle: 'In the evening there is a red lamp burning on the Cross, and from wherever I may be returning at a late hour I can see from afar this light in the dark and I know *what lies there, near that bright scarlet stain.* . . . Sometimes it has a timid air, but at other times it is unbearably terrifying in the gloom amid the snows! . . . A dread grips one—a dread for one's own self, for those nearest one, and especially for one's country, when one remembers how few such men there are in it and how soon they die, without accomplishing half of what they are capable.' Leontiev's religious vocation did not liberate him from fear; blessed peace was not for him. His religious destiny was tragic and tortured. The religious problem confronting him could not be solved in the way in which he attempted to do so. He was the martyr of a transitional religious age. His destiny was rich in lessons which might help to solve religious and philosophical problems, although he himself failed to solve them. He was the first to have a presentiment of many things. And although he was a 'reactionary', he was most sensitive to the subterranean reverberations of the impending future. But his consciousness was the prisoner of terrifying nightmares.

In the strict sense of the word, Leontiev was not a mystic. In his day there was no clear notion of the problem of mysticism as a special sphere of the spiritual life. The word 'mystical' was used in a sense almost identical with the word 'religious'. Leontiev himself used the word frequently and attached to it some great and positive value. But from his use of it we can glean no specific association other than the word 'religious' and the sense of its opposition to rationalism, materialism and so on. Leontiev's vocation was not a mystical one. He had not read the mystical literature; and there is no evidence that he had resort to mystical practice as a particular quality of spiritual experience. He never spoke of the possibility of a mystical contemplation of other worlds. His consciousness was too transcendental for that. He had no profound experience of intimacy between God and man, between God and the world. He always had a horror of the created. But in another and stricter sense mysticism is the immanency of God in the human spirit. Mysticism is profoundly occult; it is invariably the property of the inner man. Leontiev's experiences, however, may be termed exclusively transcendental and religious rather than immanent and mys-

[226]

tical. His very religiosity had something of the *Old Testament* about it. But the Biblical elements in Christianity are the least mystical ones. Thus, for all his passionate and concentrated religiosity, Leontiev had not the gift of mystical experience. His religious life was tragic but at the same time palpable and clear in all its passionate and contradictory manifestations. In this respect he presented a contrast to Vladimir Solovyev, who had the mystical gift but who was, perhaps, less passionately religious. Though not a mystic, Leontiev appreciated the value of mysticism. The fact that he was an aesthete, a lover of beauty in the world, may have been an obstacle to the mystical contemplation of the Divine mysteries of the world. His outlook on the world was essentially that of a biologist and aesthete. Once embarked upon the road of salvation, he tried to abandon and forsake the world. The mystical experience of resolving dualism in the Divine unity was unknown to him: he could not discover the way to live his religious experience in the world. He refused to grasp the fact that, however pessimistic our presentiments of the future might be, *all our spiritual strength* should be directed towards the realization of the Kingdom of God in the world, of the Divine truth in life,—in the personal as well as in the social life.

In conclusion we must distinguish which were Leontiev's strong and positive qualities, and which his weak and negative ones. Leontiev was a noble and aristocratic thinker, a champion of inequality and hierarchical order in the name of the highest cultural and aesthetic values rather than of private interests. He had little in common with practical reactionaries, just as they had little use for him. In the thirst for equality, which was spreading throughout the world, he

[227]

sensed the workings of the anti-Christian spirit, of the spirit of death and nihilism. He remained a solitary thinker whose opinions were not widely shared, whose prescience of future events was completely ignored, while attention was concentrated on the more superficial 'reactionary' elements of his thought. Long before Spengler he had grasped the fateful significance of the transformation of 'culture' into 'civilization'. Not only in his writings, but also by the example of his life, he posed the problem of the relation of Christianity to the world, to history and to culture. But he brought no solution to these problems; he remained the prisoner of a tragic dualism, of a schism within himself of Pagan and Christian elements. There was also a great deal of unresolved positivism in his pagan attitude.

We may ask what was the cause of his religious failure? He rejected humanism, and he had a certain justification for that. But he also rejected man, religiously rejected him, and therein lay his mistake. He did not conceive Christianity as the religion of the God-man and God-humanity. There was a streak of Monophysitism in his thought. He avoided man as he might avoid sin and temptation, he attached no value to man-in-himself. He wished to destroy the human element in himself, but the human element persisted, as did the immemorial paganism struggling against Christianity. Hence he was unable to follow the path of religious creativeness. But conservatism is not sufficient in itself to arrest the process of universal disintegration. A positive religious revelation was necessary to combat the false doctrines arising out of the old degenerate humanism. Leontiev's religious tragedy was a clear illustration of this fact. To-day only harm could come from a non-intelligent programme based upon Leontiev's purely 'reactionary' elements. Leontiev's thought is not suited for general consumption to-day: it cannot be 'democratized' in the cause of 'right-wing' interests. The world should be capable of producing not only a process of disintegration and death, but also one of religious and creative revival. Neither Mount Athos, Filaret, nor Optina, solved Leontiev's religious drama. His consciousness suggested no answer to the religious problem of the cosmos and mankind. He confined himself to a quest of personal salvation rather than of the Kingdom of God.

But nevertheless Leontiev survives and has a validity for our religious and social speculation. His thought is still vitally manifest in contemporary religious and philosophical currents. He remains an intellectual stimulant, a source of spiritual impulses. We should not attempt to model our thought upon his, for it is too immersed in the past; but he emerges as one of the noblest and most moving figures in Russian spiritual life.

ACADEMIC INTERNATIONAL